THE MIRACLE OF PI-WATER

Kirlian photograph of the aura radiated from ceramic embedded with Pi-water information. The black spot in the center is a 5mm-diameter ceramic ball.

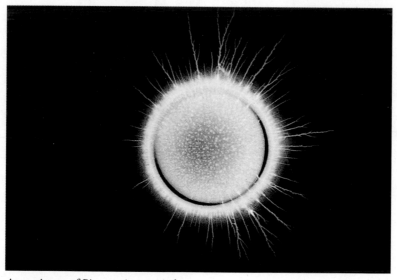

Aura picture of Pi-water in a test tube.

THIS IS WHAT PI-WATER IS.

Tuna fish were preserved in 0°C water for 20 days. The gills of fish treated with Pi-water (top) appear fresh.

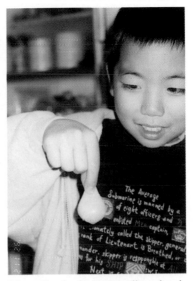

The yolk of a fresh egg will not break when picked up by hand.

6. An egg in Pi-water did not spoil after two months at room temperature (right). The other egg in untreated water decayed and became milky (left).

Hens in the Inachi poultry farm in Toyohashi City, Japan, are fed Pi-water.

AMAZING FRESHNESS RETENTION AND POLLUTION-FREE FOODS.

Carcass of swine fed by conventional methods: the meat is blotchy with congested blood.

Carcass of swine fed with Pi-water remains edible and tasty for a longer period of time.

The test area (left) was treated with Pi-water soil conditioner and a double amount of nitrogen. The control area (right) was treated in the conventional way.

Nursery boxes of rice plants, showing significant difference in growth of roots in untreated (bottom) and Pi-water-treated (top) sections.

Revival of earthworms, pond snails, and leeches.

The firm growth of roots is very important. Rice plants on the right were treated with Pi-water and soil conditioner.

HEALTHY GROWTH OF RICE PLANTS WITHOUT AGRICULTURAL CHEMICALS PRODUCES A BETTER HARVEST.

The cultivation of chemical-free melon is possible.

New sprouts shoot out from decayed dracaenas.

Seed treatment with Pi-water caused a significant difference in potato plants' growth (right).

Clear differences in the growth of hyacinth roots is apparent.

AMAZING GROWTH PROMOTED BY PI-WATER.

Healthy strawberry plants growing in soil treated with Pi-water soil conditioner.

Under conventional cultivation methods, strawberry field passages fill with water, and plant growth is poor.

Pi-water makes strong, durable concrete in which no cracks occur, thus increasing the life span of buildings.

Concrete is made from alkaline sand, such as andesite; some cracks will occur.

PI-WATER SYSTEMS IN INDUSTRIAL FIELDS.

Energy emission control system with Pi-water.

Besides improving fuel efficiency, the Pi-water system decreases a diesel engine's DEP, which is considered a cause of lung cancer.

Large-sized Pi-water processor for industrial use.

Iron pipe treated with Pi-water will not rust even when placed next to a vinyl bag (right) containing cotton soaked with concentrated hydrochloric acid. Untreated iron pipe (left) will rust quickly.

Carp, a freshwater fish, and sea bream, a seawater fish, can live together in Pi-water-treated water.

The muscle of a rat will not decay after six months in Pi-water (right).

A goldfish can live for five months in a completely sealed jar containing Pi-water.

THE POWER OF HIGH ENERGY.

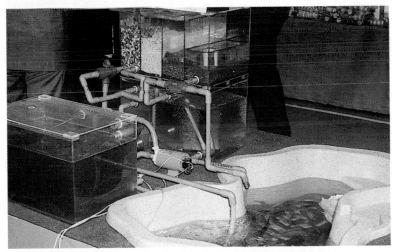

After waste water from a chicken broiler plant is filtered through a Pi-water system, the water will become clear enough for fish to live in.

Mineral water using Pi-water technology.

Cosmetics using Pi-water technology.

PI-WATER EXTENDS HEALTHY LIFE.

Pi-water purifier.

Healthy marine products in a restaurant's Pi-water tank. The treated water is brighter than other water.

A view of Mikawa Hot Spring in Mikawa Bay quasi national park, a popular Pi-water spa.

There are excellent views from the windows of the Mikawa Onsen Hotel in Mikawa Bay quasi-national park.

A GIFT FROM THE COSMOS

❀

*The revolutionary technology of water
that will save our planet and its people*

❀

THE MIRACLE OF
PI-WATER

By

Shinji Makino, Ph.D.

Translated by David Y.S. Kim, M.D., and Kazuko Kuriyama

IBE COMPANY, LTD.

NAGOYA, JAPAN

© 1999 IBE Company, Ltd.
International Standard Book Number: 0-9670571-0-8
Library of Congress Catalog Card Number: 99-71797

Published originally in Japan in 1994 by Kosaido Books
Korean edition published in 1995 by Shin Sea Dai Publishing Company

PRINTED IN THE UNITED STATES OF AMERICA

Designed and produced by Kepler Associates, Chicago, Illinois

This book is available for special promotions and premiums. Please contact the publisher for details.

IBE JAPAN
18-30, Meiekinimani 1-chome, Nakamura-ward
Nagoya, Aichi 450-0003, Japan
Telephone: 81-52-586-3161; Fax: 81-52-541-3830

℆ PI-TECH AMERICA, INC.
7300 NORTH CICERO AVENUE
LINCOLNWOOD, ILLINOIS 60712 USA
TEL: 847-675-5151, 847-675-0390; FAX: 847-763-8012

TABLE OF CONTENTS

The Wonders of Water: Essential to the Global Environment
The peculiarities of the boiling point of water, 100°C
Water is not easily heated or cooled
Ice floats on water
Water can dissolve just about anything
Water capillary phenomenon and surface tension
Water cluster
Water as a living body

The Pi-Water System Turned Around Scientific Common Sense
How Pi-Water was discovered
Basic principles of Pi-Water
The process leading to the basic principles of Pi-Water
Basic characteristics of Pi-Water
Memory retention phenomena of Pi-Water and materials
Memory retention phenomena of Pi-Water and living things
Pi-Water and heredity phenomena
Pi-Water and deionizing reaction
Fish and meat do not spoil in Pi-Water
Why the stomach wall is not affected by stomach acid
Why cholesterol adheres to the walls of blood vessels
Pi-Water and deoxidized electric potential
What is the aura?
Anybody can see *ki*
Pi-Water is the basic principle of the cosmos
Why people near the Sakurajima volcano do not have lung disease
The secret of longevity in the outer islands of Okinawa

Animals prefer to eat foods high in energy
Living creatures would perish if earth's energy becomes insufficient
Goldfish lived for five months in the sealed container
Cosmic energy was food for the goldfish
Contradiction between the training of Mt. Hiei monks and nutrition
How to identify Pi-Water
Copper-nitric acid reaction method
Dowsing
O ring test

Case reports by Dr. Harutomo Tomori, Toyo Clinic (Toyoto City, Aichi
    Prefecture)
Ms. Y, age 57, a liver cancer patient
Mr. C, age 54, a rectum cancer patient
Ms. Y, age 53, a systemic lupus erythematosus patient
Mr. A, age 53, a diabetes patient
Mr. L, age 80, a diabetes patient

Amazing effect experienced with Pi-Water
Mr. K of Niship-city, Aichi Prefecture—three years of dialysis
Mr. D. age 39, of Midori ward, Kanagawa Prefecture—Diabetes cured
    without hospitalization

Skin and hair revive with Pi-Water
Pi-Water system applied to water purifier

Environmental Pollution
Polluted water surrounding us
Enviornmental pollution and new diseases

Application of Pi-Water to our Environment
Restoring river water
Returning to nature
Pi-Water becoming known overseas
    United States
    Hungary
    Korea

Application of Pi-Water to Industrial Industries
Pi-Water effective for factory waste water treatment
Metal pipes do not rust
The strength of concrete is increased
Ocean water with Pi-Water does not freeze
Toxic waste gas from the garbage incinerator decreases

LIST OF ILLUSTRATIONS

INTRODUCTION

❀

The Pi-Water system is a unique technology, created through the study of bioscience. It is exactly the same as "life energy," which a living entity naturally possesses. The Pi-Water system is induced from a very small amount of ferric ions in the active state. The application of Pi-Water system can activate the living energy of plants and animals to promote their healthy growth. Moreover, it can improve water quality, deodorize, improve fuel efficiency, and fortify concrete among many other recognized applications.

Scientific technology has developed rapidly in the 20th century. However, it has also brought serious problems: nuclear and environmental pollution, such as destruction of the ozone layer, acid rain, and global warming. Human lives are now at risk because of the pollution of soil, water, and air. It is said that the modern science that originated in Western civilization is at a standstill. We are certain that the Pi-Water system will present solutions to these problems deriving from modern scientific technology.

The Pi-Water system is based on harmony within nature. Please note that the Pi-Water system causes not only biological activation but also nonbiological reaction in various industries. This means that the essence of this technology does not have just biological and hormonic functions. The Pi-Water system also causes changes and reactions in the level of molecules and atoms, which are the very origin of all substances. These changes indicate that there may be a new scientific technology system represented by Pi-Water, as opposed to the existing vast scientific technology system of modern science.

The application of Pi-Water system is now ahead of its basic research and studies. Basic research of the Pi-Water system has only just begun. Unfortunately, most of its principles remain unknown or unsolved at this time. We are trying our best to develop and spread the use of Pi-Water technology as quickly as we can. However, our human and monetary resources are quite limited. We must undertake research and development of the Pi-Water system on a national scale rather than undertaking it as a private project. We will strive toward further studies and applications of this exciting Pi-Water technology.

Shinji Makino, Ph.D.
September 1994

PREFACE

✿

This book is the compilation of general theory and details (appication) of Pi-Water's effects. Because of the work of Dr. Shoji Yamashita (Agricultural Department, Nagoya University) and Dr. Shinji Makino (Science Department, Tohoku University), Pi-Water has been getting much publicity and drawing people's attention lately.

Pi-Water is developed by the addition of various information from high quality natural water and ferric/ferrous salt solution. This book records evaluations of practical applications of Pi-Water in many different fields. Pi-Water's effects are known in various areas, such as agriculture, fisheries, manufacturing, and the livestock industry. It also sheds light on many problems in the medical field, which is now regarded as having been at a standstill. In fact, the book cites several examples in which Pi-Water has been extremely effective for treatment of liver cancer, rectum cancer, and various other conditions. The examples provided in this book raise many questions for current medical practices. The author, Dr. Shinji Makino, is very enthusiastic about opening the door to this new science by introducing Pi-Water into the field of physics as the bio-energy system.

In the field of human bioscience, the importance of searching for the truth based on an internal point of view is stressed. This includes nature, humans, and society—not just the external point of view that relies heavily on modern science that developed rapidly. Pi-Water is based on natural water, including sea water. Moreover, there have been no recognized side effects. These facts prove that Pi-Water goes along with the above mentioned importance.

Recently, in the field of medical science, the patient's "quality of life" began to be valued. We cannot disregard a view of life that places importance on nature.

The hologenic universe theory is widely known. It has been advocated by quantum physicists and neurophysiologists such Bohm and Pribram since the 1970s. They theorized that everything in the universe is vibrating and linked to each other and that a part of the universe includes the whole. The theory also explains that what we see as our reality is a virtual image called a hologram, created from internal order. Through a holographic model we can easily explain telepathy, supernatural phenomena, and the effects of Chinese *kiko* (a type of art used by some to prevent diseases and stay healthy by combining breathing and exercising) that we otherwise could not.

The Pi-Water system that the author advocates has a close relationship with the paradigm that exists on the contact point of science and philosophy. However, we are not yet certain what is there between the general theory (concept) and concrete examples (real effects). We must wait for future research and study. One thing that is certain is that medicine is a science in which we strive to actively involve ourselves in the dimension of the "unknown." This book is worth reading in order to educate ourselves about "new science."

Noboru Iijima, M.D.
Professor Emeritus
St. Marianna University
School of Medicine

CHAPTER ONE

❖ ❖ ❖

THE WONDERS OF WATER: ESSENTIAL TO THE GLOBAL ENVIRONMENT

THE PECULIARITIES OF THE BOILING POINT OF WATER, 100°C
Water is essential for living creatures on earth, but we often forget how important it is to us and that we cannot live without it. For example, plants need water in order to absorb nutrients such as nitrogen, phosphoric acid, and potassium. Water plays an important role in activating human cells as well as plant cells. In this section we will describe what kind of characteristics water possesses and its critical position in our daily life.

Water is a simple chemical compound, consisting only of oxygen and hydrogen. The chemical elements that belong to the same group in the periodic table normally share similar characteristics because their structure of outer electrons surrounding the atomic nucleus is similar. However, with the exception of water, the hydrogen compounds of the elements in the oxygen group, such as oxygen, sulfur, selenium, and tellurium, have very low boiling points. (See Figure 1.1: Outer Orbit of the Electron.) No one doubts that water boils at 100°C under one atmospheric pressure. However, from the physical and chemical points of view, it is a very mysterious phenomenon. Theoretically, water's boiling point should be -80°C, and the freezing point should be -110°C. But it is actually 0°C, which is exceptionally high. This is because the strength that combines water molecules

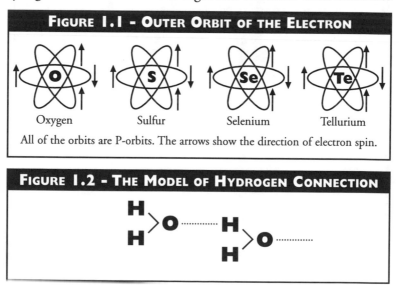

FIGURE 1.1 - OUTER ORBIT OF THE ELECTRON

Oxygen   Sulfur   Selenium   Tellurium

All of the orbits are P-orbits. The arrows show the direction of electron spin.

FIGURE 1.2 - THE MODEL OF HYDROGEN CONNECTION

(combination of hydrogen) is excessively strong. Water is described as H_2O. However, it does not exist as a single molecule of H_2O. H_2O molecules are connected to each other by a strong hydrogen combination (weak electric connection). (See Figure 1.2: The Model of Hydrogen Connection.) The steam generated by boiling water is a result of the hydrogen combination being broken.

WATER IS NOT EASILY HEATED OR COOLED

Certain areas on earth of the same latitude may be quite different in climate depending upon their particular locations. For example, Madrid, Spain, and Aomori, Japan, are both about 40 degrees north in latitude, but whereas the average yearly temperature in Madrid is 14.3°C, it is only 9.7°C in Aomori. It is believed that the difference is due to ocean currents. While the climate in Madrid is influenced by a warm ocean current, the climate in Aomori is affected by a cold ocean current.

Heat capacity of the ocean current is so significant that it affects average temperatures in certain areas. How could water have such heat capacity? It is because the specific heat, or heat capacity, of water is much greater than that of other substances. (See Table 1.1: Specific Heat of Different Substances (cal/g. deg).) Specific heat is defined as the calories necessary to raise the tem-

TABLE 1.1 – SPECIFIC HEAT OF DIFFERENT SUBSTANCES (CAL/G. DEG)	
Water	1.00
Methanol	0.60
Ethanol	0.68
N-Butyl Alcohol	0.56
Asphalt	0.22
Stone	about 0.2
Sand	0.19
Wood	0.45-0.65

The above figures are at normal room temperature.

perature of certain substances by one degree Celsius, and its unit measure is cal/g C. For example, if you put a piece of iron in the flame of fire, it would be heated right away to a point at which you could not touch it with your hand. However, water in an iron pot would not be heated so quickly. This is because the heat capacity of water is greater.

In a desert the difference between daytime temperature and nighttime temperature could be as much as 50°C. If you were standing on a sand hill in the setting sun and put one foot in the sun and the other in the shade, the one in the sun would become burning hot, while the other in the shade would be quite cool.

The reason these phenomena occur is that the evaporation heat of water is 539.8 calories per 1 gram, which is considerably greater than that of other substances, and its coagulation heat is also greater—at 79.7 calories. This means that in an environment containing water, the temperature is kept within the moderate range, whereas in the environment without water, such as the desert, it gets hot or cold suddenly. Water, indeed, plays an important role in regulating temperature.

ICE FLOATS ON WATER

It is a well known fact that ice floats on water, but this phenomenon is very abnormal from the standpoint of physics and chemistry. Generally, when liquid is cooled, its weight per 1 cc (specific gravity) becomes heavier as the temperature goes down. The same property applies to water. However, water starts to become lighter at 4°C, and even lighter as it turns into ice with the temperature going further down. Eventually, ice floats on water as the result. (See Graph1.1: Temperature and Specific Gravity of Water (g/cm³).) Conversely, pure acetic acid begins to coagulate at 16.7°C, and the portion that coagulates earlier sinks at the bottom. We can see this separation clearly.

Water is the only substance that in its frozen state becomes lighter than its original liquid state. If the specific gravity of ice were heavier than that of water, ice would sink to the bottom of the ocean. The surface of the ocean would become warm, which

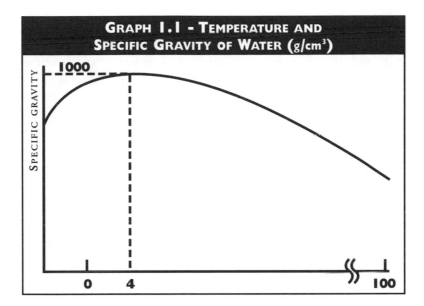

would lead to disastrous consequences for the environment. It is the unique properties of water that allowed life to develop.

WATER CAN DISSOLVE JUST ABOUT ANYTHING

Water's capacity to dissolve other substances is exceptionally high. Interestingly, after dissolving one substance, water can still dissolve others. For example, after water has dissolved carbon dioxide, it can dissolve calcium, other minerals, and organic matter. A detergent containing a surface activating agent can even dissolve oil, which cannot be dissolved in plain water.

WATER CAPILLARY PHENOMENON AND SURFACE TENSION

Suppose we place one end of a towel in a bucket of water and let the other end hang out of it. We will find that water will flow out of the bucket through the towel. This is called a capillary phenomenon of water, and the towel, in this case, acts as capillary tubes. The capillary phenomenon in soil is important because it carries water to the root of plants. If water did not have this capillary property, then rain falling on the surface of the earth would not penetrate underground. Thus, plants would not be able to absorb water. Moreover, water would not evaporate from the surface of the earth, which would make it impossible to control the temperature of the earth.

Liquids also have surface tension. Surface tension accounts for the spherical shape of liquid drops. The surface tension of water is much higher than that of other liquids. The higher the surface tension of a liquid is, the higher that liquid rises in the capillary tubes with the capillary phenomenon. Thus, capillary phenomenon and/or surface tension plays an important role in many phenomena of nature.

WATER CLUSTER

As mentioned earlier, molecules of water are connected by a hydrogen combination. Water does not exist as a single molecule of H_2O, but instead forms a string of H_2Os. This group of H_2O molecules is called a water cluster. Unfortunately, the size of water clusters cannot be accurately measured at the present time. However, it is generally determined by measuring half the width of ^{17}O-NMR (nuclear magnet resonance spectrum). The smaller the value, the smaller the cluster of water. (See Graph 1.2: ^{17}O-NMR Half Width.)

Recently, there has been much talk about "water clusters." Originally, the concept of clusters came from the research and studies for the Japanese rice wine industry. Mature rice wine has

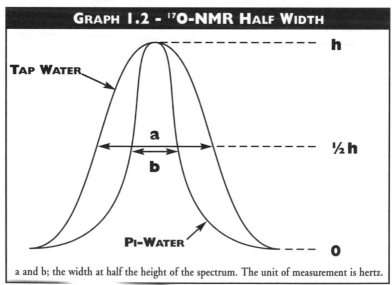

GRAPH 1.2 - ^{17}O-NMR HALF WIDTH

a and b; the width at half the height of the spectrum. The unit of measurement is hertz.

a mild taste and would not cause any bad side effects in comparison with immature rice wine. However, there is no difference between the two as far as alcohol content, sugar content, and other ingredients are concerned when chemically analyzed. Further study disclosed that the water cluster in mature rice wine is smaller. In other words, the physical characteristics of the water molecule in mature rice wine is different. After this finding, researchers concluded that water with smaller clusters is healthier. However, it has not yet been medically proven.

WATER AS A LIVING BODY

Since more than 60 percent of the human body is water, it can be said without exaggeration that water holds the key to life. When thinking about health, many people pay attention to medicine and food. Only a few pay much attention to water. However, it is water that is most important. According to Darwin's theory of evolution, life began in the ocean. This theory explains why the composition of bodily liquid (living body water) is almost the same as sea water. (See Table 1.2: Comparison of Iron Concentration Within Bodily Fluid and Ocean Water.)

When we inject medication into the human body, we use saline solution, which can be compared to sea water diluted to 25 percent. When injected, the person feels very little pain. However, if purified water were injected, the mineral would have been taken out of the water through an iron exchange process, and the person would feel severe pain. Unlike saline water, the ion balance of purified water is not in order.

TABLE 1.2 - COMPARISON OF IRON CONCENTRATION WITHIN BODILY FLUID AND OCEAN WATER					
	Na^+	K^+	Ca^{2+}	Mg^{2+}	Cl^-
Ocean water	100	3.61	3.91	12.1	181
Bodily fluid of human	100	6.75	3.10	0.70	129
Human blood	100	6.00	2.67	11.0	164

(Comparative figures with Na⁺ being 100.)

Water freezes at 0°C, but saline solution does not. The reason that saline solution does not freeze at 0°C is not merely because there is mineral and ion dissolved in it, but also because it is structured as "water in crevice" within a cell. For example, suppose we have 0.001mm in between two pieces of glass and put some water between them, the water in crevice does not freeze at -100°C.

CHAPTER TWO

❖ ❖ ❖

THE
PI-WATER SYSTEM
TURNED AROUND
SCIENTIFIC
COMMON SENSE

HOW PI-WATER WAS DISCOVERED

Pi-Water was discovered during the study of the physiology of plants. As we know, some plants flower in spring. Generally, the buds that become flowers and those that become leaves are the same. We observe a bud as it emerges, thinking that it will become a leaf when spring comes; surprisingly, it turns out to be a flower instead. This is called the differentiation of flower buds. Many scholars studying this phenomenon hypothesized that there is a hormone within plants that turns buds into flowers. They named this hormone *florigen,* the "flower maker."

In Japan the late professor Yoshiaki Goto and Dr. Shoji Yamashita of the agricultural department of Nagoya University devoted themselves to studying florigen. Unfortunately, they could not isolate it. However, in 1964 during their study, they discovered that the living water contained in plants plays an important role in flower bud differentiation.

Further research revealed that the living water was totally different from well or tap water both in its physical characteristics and biological activities. In 1985 Dr. Yamashita tentatively named this water *Pi-Water.* Therefore, the original definition of Pi-Water is "the water that is very similar to living water." Later, researchers noted that Pi-Water also plays an important role in the healthy growth of plants and animals, not just in flower bud differentiation.

Recent studies established that Pi-Water is induced by a very small amount of iron ions. These iron ions found in Pi-Water are ferric ferrous ions that are in a highly energized state.

BASIC PRINCIPLES OF PI-WATER

As illustrated in Figure 2.1: Hypothetical Mechanism of Pi-Water System, it is interesting to note that the use of Pi-Water can contribute to the healthy growth of plants and animals as well as to a wide variety of different applications, such as maintaining freshness of fish, improving soil conditions, preventing metals from rusting, fortifying concrete, improving fuel oil and its efficiency, preventing electric charge, and purifying water.

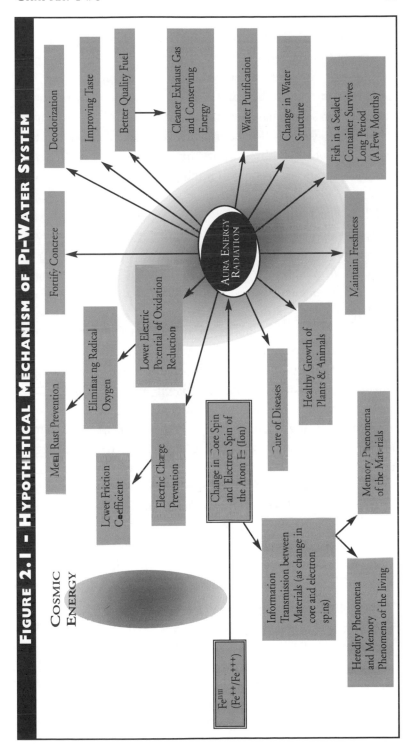

Figure 2.1 – Hypothetical Mechanism of Pi-Water System

What kind of mechanism does Pi-Water have that leads to such unique characteristics?

Since the Pi-Water system has such a profound meaning, its application preceded the basic studies. Unfortunately, the basic studies and research have just begun, and most of the principles of Pi-Water system still remain in the dark. We shall attempt to set forth a bold hypothesis about the principles of Pi-Water system. Please read on, keeping in mind that the basic proof has not yet been made.

When ferric/ferrous salt (Fe $^{II/III}$) receives cosmic energy waves, a change occurs in the nuclear and electron spin of the iron atom that causes the atom to be in a highly energized state. The highly energized iron atom radiates electromagnetic waves, or *auras*. These electromagnetic waves, or auras, are the essence of Pi-Water. (See Figure 2.1: Hypothetical Mechanism of Pi-Water System.)

With the changes in nuclear and electron spin, information can be transferred between substances. These changes can also affect the memory phenomena of substances and, therefore, the genetic material of living beings. Based on this principle, Pi-Water can easily be influenced by an electromagnetic field.

What causes the "cosmic energy" from which the ferric/ferrous salt (Fe $^{II/III}$) receives its waves? The answer has remained largely unsolved. Its unknown energy waves fill the vast space of the cosmos. Many people from ancient times had pointed out its existence.

In August 1991 the 26th Congress of Energy Conversion Engineering was held in Boston. This annual conference was an international event sponsored by seven different academic societies, such as the U.S. Atomic Energy Society, Electric Engineering Society, and Machine Engineering Society. In this event the Innovative Energy Division was established. There were thirty presentations regarding such topics as cosmic energy and cosmic energy generators.

Although cosmic energy is finally becoming recognized internationally, it is unfortunate that there are no organized studies carried out yet by any country on a national scale. In any case, the Pi-Water system must be very closely related to cosmic system.

THE PROCESS LEADING TO THE BASIC PRINCIPLES OF PI-WATER

The Mössbauer spectrum is used as a means of assessing the condition of Fe electron spin. When we measured the Mössbauer spectrum from ferric/ferrous salt of Pi-Water, we found the electrons of Fe spinning rapidly, which means that they contain high energy.

Extreme infrared radiation is known to prevent food spoiling and odor and to promote growth of plants. These effects are similar to those of Pi-Water. We suspected that Pi-Water might emit extreme infrared radiation, so we measured the radiation rate of a sodium chloride crystal of Pi-Water. To our surprise, the radiation rate became clearly lower than before. Normally, every substance has its own fixed rate of extreme infrared radiation. Therefore, the extreme infrared radiation rate of sodium chloride from Pi-Water should be fixed and should not change. On the other hand, the evidence of extreme change in the infrared radiation rate means that the energy of ferric/ferrous salt was somehow transferred and retained in sodium chloride.

The fact that the extreme infrared radiation rate of sodium chloride crystal became considerably lower shows that energy was released in a form other than extreme infrared radiation. We presume that this energy difference is emitted as *aura energy*.

In order to confirm about how much aura energy is actually released, we took a Kirlian photograph of Pi-Water. (Kirlian photography captures a photographic image of what is considered to be aura energy.) We were able to see a beautiful and strong aura emerging from Pi-Water's ceramics, an aura that looked like fireworks. When we took a photo of Pi-Water in a test tube, we also saw a strong aura emission from the Pi-Water itself. We were told that when psychic people see Pi-Water, they may see an aura reaching as high as 30 to 40 cm.

BASIC CHARACTERISTICS OF PI-WATER

Pi-Water is:

Water containing aura energy (energy of a living entity);
Water containing undulating movement;

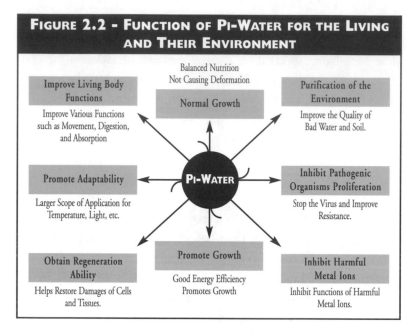

An energy system of the living entity;

Material information transmission and memory system;

A system that changes cosmic energy into aura (energy among energy), the basic principles of the universe. (See Figure 2.2: Function of Pi-Water for the Living and Their Environment.)

Pi-Water, which we may refer to as "the water of the twenty-first century," will bring considerable changes to our lives in the future.

MEMORY RETENTION PHENOMENA OF PI-WATER
AND MATERIALS

The earth was formed about 4.6 billion years ago. Since that time, it is said that the earth's axis has changed its angle several times. This means that the present North and South Poles are not in the same positions that they were when the earth was formed. For example, fossils of mammoths have been found in Siberia, which suggests the possibility that the present North Pole was close to the tropics millions of years ago. We discovered the earth's axis had changed a long time ago because some rocks have retained the information of the angle of the earth's axis (terrestrial magnetism).

The following are some examples of memory retention phenomena in different substances:

- Observing the stump of a tree, we can tell how old the tree is or the climate of a particular year, because the information is expressed in the annual rings.
- Analyzing a section of a building, for example, part of the pillar in Horyuji temple in Japan, by isotope analysis, tells us when the structure was built because the information is retained as the composition ratio of the carbon isotope.
- Studying a single human hair allows us to presume his or her blood type, age, personality, and even diet to a certain degree. If we can detect medications in the hair, we can also learn what kinds of diseases he or she may have suffered from.
- Examining a glass of wine, a specialist should be able to analyze the variety of grape, when the wine was made, and the quality of the grape crop in that year.
- Inspecting a piece of earthenware tells us what technology and material was used in its manufacture as well as the temperature at which it was baked.
- Testing a seemingly straight iron bar, we can tell how many times and how hard it has been bent in the past or the condition of its metal fatigue.
- Analyzing water reveals its memory retention ability. Scientific common sense states that liquids cannot be magnetized; however, water that has passed through a magnetic field (magnetic water) clearly shows changes in biological activation. This certainly means that water retains the memory that it has passed through a magnetic field.

Various substances thus store accurate information about their histories. A stone on the street may be packed with various information and may even "remember" that it was kicked by a pretty lady with an umbrella on such and such date, which was a rainy day. However, with present scientific technology, we are still unable to read the information accurately enough.

Nevertheless, materials retain information, such as physical changes, crystal and molecular structural modifications, scientific formations, and atomic electron and core spin.

Water may also demonstrate changes. If water goes through a Pi-Water system purifier, its clusters become extremely small. This change occurs because Pi-ceramic releases aura energy that breaks down the hydrogen connections. When we try to see this phenomenon from the standpoint of information retention, the information of the original Pi-Water is retained in the Pi-ceramic and is then transferred to the water. This means that changes in the electron spin of ferric/ferrous salt cause changes in the electron spin of the atoms that are included in the ceramic. These changes, in turn, cause changes in the water, and then finally the information is retained as the structural changes of that water.

MEMORY RETENTION PHENOMENA OF PI-WATER
AND LIVING THINGS

Flowers bloom in spring. Where does the plant retain the information that it is supposed to bloom in springtime? It is the living water(Pi-Water) in the plant structure. The information is probably retained as the change in the electron spin-off of ferric/ferrous ($Fe^{II/III}$). Extremely small amounts of these electrons are contained in living body water.

A carrier pigeon returns to its own nest from a place several hundred kilometers away. A salmon comes back to the river where it was born after traveling thousands of kilometers. Many biologists have studied and tried to understand the mystery behind the behavior of these animals One scientist claimed that he had found a magnet in a pigeon's brain, though this is still in dispute. It makes more sense to presume that Pi-Water's memory retention system is functioning in the body of a carrier pigeon or a salmon.

PI-WATER AND HEREDITY PHENOMENA

The most typical example of memory retention phenomena in living things is heredity. The study of gene recombination is quite advanced now. Recently, approval was granted in the United

States to distribute tomatoes made through gene recombination . However, many people oppose this new practice because of their concern about the effects gene recombination could have on living substances.

The gene is substance through which a parent conveys various characteristics to its offspring. The basic material of the gene is DNA (deoxyribonucleic acid), which is the combination of the macromolecules adenine, cytosine, guanine, and thymine that are combined in two chains and in a spiral.

The genetic information of a gene that is conveyed from a parent to an offspring is double-spiral DNA copied by RNA, which plays a messenger's role. Copying is carried out by a kind of enzyme called DNA polymerase. Polymerase has an amazingly accurate ability to copy and reproduce. Its accuracy can be compared to copying a billion or so letters and making only one mistake. However, the level of accuracy depends on the environment of the living body.

DNA theory has already been proven and established. When we go one step further and suppose that there may be some other material that plays an important part in this DNA information transmission, we cannot dispute the importance of iron. DNA is three-dimensionally structured protein with the double helix figure and has the width of 20 angstrom (1 angstrom = 10^8 cm). We think that the functions such as information transmission and copying are controlled by iron and that other substances such as DNA only help them achieve their goals.

There are actual examples of heredity phenomena related to Pi-Water. For instance, seed rice treated with Pi-Water shows excellent growth after germination. When first-generation seed rice are sown, they grow very well. Then, when rice is produced again and used as second generation seed rice, they again grow quite well. This could happen because the form and nature of heredity have changed. On the other hand, if we use a sufficient amount of fertilizer, such as nitrogen, phosphoric acid, and potassium, as is done conventionally, the growth of plants certainly improves; however, the seed rice that is produced does not grow as well. This is because the form and nature of heredity remains the same.

It is possible that protein does not convey the hereditary information, but instead the iron (Fe) on the DNA or RNA transmits the heredity information. It is assumed that DNA and RNA merely create the environment that makes it easier for a gene's copying work to be done.

Some may say that the transmission of information carried out by a gene is scientifically proven and that Fe does not exist. However, with modern science it is difficult to eliminate iron (Fe) completely. Even if we carry out ion exchange or distilling, we definitely still have a very small amount of iron ions. Therefore, we cannot completely deny the involvement of a small amount of iron in the heredity phenomenon.

Another example of the heredity phenomenon in plants is reported by Professor Yoshiaki Goto of the Agriculture Department of Nagoya University and Dr. Shoji Yamashita. They treated the seeds of a variety of radish called twenty-day radish, which would normally flower under spring (long day) conditions, with Pi-Water that retains autumn (short day) conditions in its memory. These seeds germinated and grew and then also flowered during short-day conditions.

The reason that flowers bloom in spring or autumn depends on the heredity form and nature that the seeds possess. However, the experiment conducted at Nagoya University shows that the heredity form and nature changed. Heredity phenomena are said to be controlled by genes. We assume that this is the truth, yet in the above experiment the fact that cytoplasmic heredity without genes can exist makes us reconsider what heredity really means.

PI-WATER AND DEIONIZING REACTION

It is said that Pi-Water has a deionizing function. Here are several phenomena that prove it:

- No "fur" (soap film) on the bathtub. If you take a look at the bathtub in the morning after four or five people have taken baths (in the Japanese style, that is) during the previous evening, you might see quite a bit of fur, or scum, along the water line. It is not easy to get rid of the fur by just flushing it with water or scrubbing it with your fingers. Although scum is not physically stuck on the wall of the tub, it is stuck to the tub through electrostatically generated magnetic poles.

If you use a Pi-Water system in your bathtub, you would perhaps still have fur, but it would not stick to the tub. If you were to flush the tub with Pi-Water, you could wash off the fur easily, even without detergent because Pi-Water deionizes, or removes, the electrical charges from the water.

- No more dirty and slimy drainage pipes. The inside of drainage pipes in a bathroom or kitchen are very dirty and slimy. If you used Pi-Water in these pipes, you would not have the same problem for the same reasons, namely, that you would not have electrically charged scum on the wall of the bathtub.

- No bad smell in the room. If you spray Pi-Water in a smelly room, the bad smell disappears immediately. Human beings sense the smell when the substance that causes the smell (molecules) is combined with the cell for the sense of smell. Then that information is conveyed to the brain as electrical stimulation. Therefore, in order to be able to sense the smell, the substance causing the smell must have electrically separate poles. When we spray Pi-Water, it suppresses these molecules from being separated into two poles, thus making the odor disappear.

- Electric conductivity becomes considerably lower. To find out how much chemical fertilizer is present in soil, we measure the soil's electric conductivity (EC). Chemical fertilizer is separated into positive ions and negative ions in the water contained in soil. The more ions the soil contains, the higher the EC. If the EC is too high, there can be problems for the crops. However, if we treat the soil with Pi-Water, the high EC rate drops rapidly from 4.0 to about 3.0. Having lowered EC by 1.0 means that the ion concentration dropped by one digit. This phenomenon is quite significant in agriculture and can be interpreted as a deionizing function of Pi-Water. It is also believed that when receiving the aura energy of Pi-Water, chemical fertilizer contents combine with the soil structure and cause them not to function as separate ions.

If this were a physical, that is, chemical deionizing, phenomenon only, then Pi-Water's hydrogen ion concentration rate (pH) should always be 7.0 and the EC should be zero. However, in reality, this is not the case, and the rates do not go down.

We presume the above phenomena occur because the energy level of the molecule receiving aura energy from Pi-Water increases and changes the reaction pattern.

FISH AND MEAT DO NOT SPOIL IN PI-WATER

While in Pi-Water, a piece of pig's lung tissue did not spoil for six months at room temperature. In addition, if we break an egg into a container of Pi-Water, it can remain completely unspoiled for two months at room temperature. Place that same egg in regular tap water, and it will spoil within two weeks. Fresh fish reacts the same. How can one explain why this happens?

Generally, some think that Pi-Water has a sterilizing function or suppresses bacteria so spoiling does not occur quite so soon. However, the results of testing showed that Pi-Water does not have such capabilities.

Striped shellfish was put in Pi-Water, kept at room temperature, and imported to Japan. The shellfish was quite fresh upon its arrival. However, Japanese customs officials rejected it. When fresh, uncooked seafood goes through customs, it is inspected for coliform and various kinds of bacteria. The above mentioned striped shellfish did not pass that inspection. Although the shellfish was fresh, it had coliform and other kinds of germs. What does this mean?

Generally it is considered that foods spoil because bacteria within the food multiply. However, this theory may not be totally correct. There certainly were some germs on the shellfish, but they did not multiply, and the shellfish did not spoil. We believe that the following may have happened.

Live tissue, particularly protein, retains an extremely complicated three-dimensional (3-D) structure. While this 3-D structure is maintained, it cannot be attacked by bacteria. However, when the tissue dies and loses its aura energy, its 3-D structure collapses, making it susceptible to bacteria attack. Therefore, it is believed that the 3-D structure itself in the living tissue prevents the attack of bacteria. It is probably living energy (aura energy) in the Pi-Water that maintains this 3-D structure. Thus, we understand the reason why a raw egg and a piece of fresh fish do not spoil in Pi-Water.

On the other hand, if you import striped shellfish that has been sterilized with chlorine and received at normal unrefrigerated temperature from the Philippines, it may arrive in Japan without any coliform or any other kind of bacteria. However, the shellfish itself would be completely melted or disintegrated. It would melt by itself due to an enzyme that the living tissue itself possesses to break down the protein.

WHY THE STOMACH WALL IS NOT AFFECTED BY STOMACH ACID
Human stomach acid, which normally shows a hydrogen ion concentration rate (pH) of 1.6 to 2.0 is quite strong. When protein comes in contact with such strong acid, it would normally change its characteristics or decompose. However, the stomach wall is not affected. This is a strange phenomenon. It is generally thought that the stomach is not affected because it is covered with a protective mucous membrane that consists of protein.

It may be easier to understand that tissue with strong bio-energy is maintaining the 3-D structure that it should have and thus is not affected by stomach acid. In fact, it is evident that animal tissue would not change its characteristics or decompose when placed into Pi-Water with pH 1.0 to 2.0.

WHY CHOLESTEROL ADHERES TO THE WALLS OF BLOOD VESSELS
People who have high blood pressure worry about cholesterol and neutral lipid (fat) concentration in the blood when they reach middle age. They are worried because these substances form deposits on the wall of the blood vessels, leading to arteriosclerosis. People with

high blood pressure therefore try to stay away from meat and various sea foods that contain high cholesterol and fat.

When a young, healthy person eats food with high cholesterol, it does not adhere to the wall of his or her blood vessels. However, if a middle-aged or an older person eats these types of food, the fats may create deposits on the wall of the blood vessels. One might wonder, how is this possible?

It is clear from our previous discussion that soap film adheres to the bathtub because of static electricity. If we use Pi-Water, scum will not stick on the tub walls because Pi energy (aura) suppresses static electricity. It has been suggested that cholesterol deposits on the blood vessel walls are due to static electricity. Thus, cholesterol (or neutral fat) deposits do not occur in blood vessels of a young, healthy person because bio-energy (aura energy) suppresses the cholesterol adherence caused by static electricity.

PI-WATER AND DEOXIDIZED ELECTRIC POTENTIAL

Pi-Water, especially high energy Pi-Water, shows extremely low deoxidized electric potential. By putting just three drops of Pi-Water into 150 ml of regular tap water that has deoxidized electric potential of +180mV, the water's electric potential drops to –35mV. Therefore, Pi-Water has a very strong deoxidizing capability.

Pi-Water has a natural deoxidizing function, and it suppresses the oxidizing function. It suppresses not only radical oxygen but also prevents rust on metals and the oxidizing of processed food. Lower deoxidizing electric potential means Pi-Water plays an important role in human health and cosmetic manufacturing.

Aging is caused mainly by radical oxygen and lipid peroxide. Pi-Water can suppress the harmful consequences of these changes. The mechanism to lower the deoxidizing electric potential has much to do with the aura energy that Pi-Water emits as well as ferric/ferrous ($Fe^{II/III}$) themselves. Radical oxygen is a big enemy to your skin, and Pi-Water can suppress it. That's why it becomes an important ingredient in the cosmetics industry.

WHAT IS THE AURA?

People say. "An aura is surrounding him." What exactly is an aura?

You are undoubtedly familiar with pictures of Christ or statues of Buddha. Portrayed above the head of Jesus Christ is a white ring and behind Buddha a golden light that we refer to as a halo. These are auras. The color and shape of an aura depends upon the person it surrounds. The common conception is that this is living energy.

Recently people started paying more attention to auras as something that reflects human consciousness. According to people who can see auras, the color differs depending on the individual person. It also changes when he or she is relaxed or becomes angry. When two people who get along well are together, their auras are mixed and have a similar color. However, when a divorced couple or family members who do not communicate well are together, there are dark lines between the auras of the individuals. When you meet someone for the first time and you find that he or she is the type you do not like, your aura waves are conveyed to him or her as soon as you feel that way. Thus, your consciousness becomes energy, which is released from your body as your aura. There is no concept of time and space with consciousness, so your aura is conveyed to the other person as soon as you have a thought.

Let's talk about something more common. There are many ways to improve health these days. Some people are trying to learn healing therapies (*kiko* or *tai kyoku ken*, for example) that deal with the power of *ki,* or spiritual energy. Some doctors in Japan and the United States use spiritual energy (*ki*) and meditation as part of their medical practice, and some of them have actually helped their AIDS and cancer patients to heal. However, this *ki* cannot be scientifically explained. The best modern science can do to illustrate *ki* is to monitor temperature changes in the person emitting *ki* and in the person receiving it or to observe brain waves such as alpha waves.

You may have seen the following on television. A Chinese *kiko* master, Ms. Shaojin, radiated *ki* or spiritual energy for just a few minutes to a patient suffering from an incurable disease and who could not even walk. After treatment this patient not only began to walk but also ran a little afterward. This experiment was conducted with doctors from St. Marianna University School of Medicine as witnesses, so there was legitimate proof.

Another *kiko* master can move a candle flame placed on the other side of a glass screen and can also throw someone without using his hands. He can do all these things by radiating his *ki* energy. Some people can use *ki* from birth without any practice; however, all people can radiate *ki* if they train themselves. This *ki* is called an aura.

ANYBODY CAN SEE *KI*

Even without practice, anybody can generate *ki*. There is a simple experiment that proves that. First, fill two glasses with tap water that contains chlorine. Then, into one of the glasses, put two or three drops of a chlorine detection reagent called orthotrizine, which you can buy at a pharmacy. The water in that glass should change to yellow immediately. If you are in an area such as Tokyo where the chlorine content of tap water is very high, the water may even turn brown.

Next, place your index and middle fingers of your right hand all the way into the second glass. Keep them in the glass for one minute, and then take them out. Place two or three drops of orthotrizine in the second glass.

If you have strong *ki*, the water will not turn yellow. The *ki* energy suppresses the oxidizing reaction of chlorine, which is why the color does not change. If your body energy is not sufficient to suppress the chlorine, then the color changes to yellow. As you can see from this experiment, everyone generates *ki*.

An aura is not generated just from living bodies but from substances as well. For example, sacred places have aura energy that attracts people. They do not have aura energy because people gather there. Some mountains have auras, and some do not. What is the source of aura energy for living bodies or substances? All living bodies or substances take in cosmic energy that exists in the space around them and then radiate it outward.

PI-WATER IS THE BASIC PRINCIPLE OF THE COSMOS

About 4.6 billion years ago, many meteorites crashed into the earth. With the heat generated from those collisions, the earth, also a meteorite during this stage of its development, melted and became like a fireball. As the earth absorbed smaller meteorites and grew larger, it began to develop a stronger gravitational force, attracting many meteorites to itself.

The meteorite that became earth was a compound of carbon, nitrogen, and hydrogen. A very small amount of water contained in the meteorite evaporated and surrounded the earth. It rained on the lava on the ground causing it to cool and form an ocean.

There were harmful ultraviolet rays from the sun coming to the earth at that time that made it impossible for the environment to sustain any form of life. Then, hydrogen sulfide from the ocean created life. This new life used the sun and carbon dioxide in the process of photosynthesis to generate oxygen. Thus, the oxygen of the present earth was formed. Amino acids played an important role in this beginning of life, and it is thought that they may have been contained in the meteorite.

In a 1953 experiment Dr. Harold Urey of the University of Chicago developed amino acids similar to those that helped originate life. He assembled the same ingredients the earth had in its beginning—carbon dioxide, ammonia, and water—and discharged electricity for one week. As a result, amino acids were successfully created. His experiment proved that amino acids, which were considered to be made only from living entities, could be made in the earth in its beginning. Later on, amino acids were found in the meteorite that fell in the suburbs of Melbourne, Australia, in 1969, which proved that they can certainly be made in the natural world as well.

The earth in its beginning was full of cosmic energy, more than we can ever imagine. It is considered that the minerals on the earth generated aura energy. It is the same aura energy that Pi-Water possesses. The combination of substance and energy was perfect in the earth in its beginning, and so it was possible for life to begin.

About 3.8 billion years ago when life began, the earth was full of aura energy (Pi energy), and various kinds of living plants and animals grew extremely well. The energy that the earth had at that time still remains in the earth's interior liquid rock called the magma, which has a tremendous amount of energy. Magma energy continues to be emitted even now and is received and used by various substances and creatures on earth.

WHY PEOPLE NEAR THE SAKURAJIMA VOLCANO DO NOT HAVE LUNG DISEASE

Every time Sakurajima erupts in Kagoshima, Japan, the city is covered with more than 20 cm of volcanic ash per day. While driving, you cannot see in front of you even with the headlights on. Furthermore, you cannot help inhaling a small amount of volcanic ash if you live there. Nevertheless, the average life expectancy in Kagoshima is age 79, which is quite high. Moreover, the number of those who suffer from respiratory diseases, such as pneumonia, is much lower than that of other cities. If you regard volcanic ash just as a kind of dust, it is a negative factor for your health. However, its positive factor overcomes the negative because the ashes are from underground magma that carries Pi energy.

THE SECRET OF LONGEVITY IN THE OUTER ISLANDS OF OKINAWA

Many people living on the outer islands of Okinawa grow sugar cane. They mainly engage in agriculture or fishing, working from early in the morning until late at night. On some of the islands, there are no adequate medical facilities. There may only be one doctor who makes monthly visits. Life there is so much more primitive compared to that of city dwellers; however, they live much longer than those who live in the cities. What is the secret behind their longevity?

People on the islands use well water. Underground water on these islands is filtered through layers of coral-limestone soil. The layer of coral is that of fossil coral, which has extremely high energy. By drinking this water everyday, the islanders are drinking energized water. However, the secret of their longevity is generally considered to be a result of dissolved calcium in the well water. Another example: The contents of the water of Lourdes in France are not different from regular water, but people drink it and are able to cure their diseases. How can we explain this phenomenon?

Animals prefer to eat foods high in energy

The earth is a mass of energy, and living animals and plants on earth receive this energy. This has been going on continuously since 3.8 billion years ago when life began on earth. For example, in ancient times plants such as ferns grew extremely well. However, it was not just because there was sufficient nitrogen, phosphoric acid, and potassium in the soil to promote their growth.

We eat energy in food everyday. Of course, nutrition such as vitamins matters, but on the whole, energy plays a larger part. Recently, vegetables have been widely grown in greenhouses, where there is very little energy in the soil. Thus, there are smaller amounts of nutrients and less energy contained in them. However, this energy can be obtained from sources other than foods. When you walk through the forest, you feel relaxed and comfortable, because you breathe in the energy radiated by plants through breathing. Wild animals first eat the organs of their game. When some native peoples in Africa, South East Asia, and South America catch their game and share it, the leader and heroes within the tribe have the first right to eat the organs. They know that the organs have concentrated energy.

Living creatures would perish if earth's energy becomes insufficient

Everything in the natural world lives, receiving the blessing of the earth's aura energy. All the animals, plants, and minerals once shared energy equally. However, the chemical substances produced by human beings function in such a way as to destroy the earth energy.

By using too much chemical fertilizer and agricultural chemicals, we reduce the productivity of the soil rapidly, squandering its energy. We continue to grow crops in such weak soil that we need more chemicals and chemical fertilizer to make the soil more effective.

Detergent that we use everyday also contaminates the water in our rivers, which drains the energy the water used to have. The air is also polluted with exhaust from automobiles and power plants and is losing its energy rapidly.

Agricultural chemicals decrease the soil's energy, and chemicals used as medicine and food additives decrease human natural healing power. It is ideal to eat organically grown foods if you want to obtain energy from them. We need to supply soil, water, and air with strong energy in order to keep them as clean as they used to be long ago. Unless we do so now, we cannot replenish the aura energy fast enough to keep up with the rate that the environment is deteriorating, which would have catastrophic effects on the earth.

Leading a healthy life leads to recovering the earth's environment. We must make the soil, water, and air clean. It would take 500 to 1,000 years to regenerate the earth's natural environment as it used to be, even if each one of us becomes careful and tries to lead a healthy life. We cannot imagine that the earth will maintain the present condition until then.

As mentioned earlier, the essence of Pi-Water is strong energy waves, the same as aura and *ki* energy. There is an unlimited amount of cosmic energy existing around us. By using Pi-Water, which works as a transforming agent, we can change this energy into the kind of energy that living beings can use. It can be very effective, depending upon how we use it. The principle of Pi-Water was found in the physiological study of plants. It is not a substance that human beings have created. Considering this, Pi-Water must be one of the most effective energies to revive our natural world.

GOLDFISH LIVED FOR FIVE MONTHS IN THE SEALED CONTAINER

If we were to put a goldfish in a container of dechlorinated tap water and seal it, the goldfish would die of oxygen deficiency within 24 hours. However, if we were to do the same experiment with Pi-Water, the goldfish would live for two or three months. There is nothing else in the container, such as grass or food. Once

Figure 2.3: A goldfish lived five months in the sealed container filled with Pi-Water.

in our laboratory, we had a goldfish living for five months in Pi-Water (See Figure 2.3: A goldfish lived five months in the sealed container filled with Pi-Water.). The phenomenon that a goldfish can continue to live in a small, sealed container presents a major issue to us: What is breathing? What is life?

Modern science, including medicine, cannot explain why a goldfish continues to live without oxygen or food. Then how can we explain this?

To begin, what is breathing? It is just a means of obtaining living energy. A goldfish is swimming in Pi-Water, which is aura energy, living energy itself. This goldfish can obtain living energy without any effort, since it is in a "sea" of living energy. Therefore, it does not need to breathe and does not need oxygen. If you think this way, you can understand why a goldfish continues to live in a sealed container. However, the goldfish is swimming around and it must be using up quite a lot of energy. Even if Pi-Water is living energy itself, the energy within the container should decrease by the same amount as the energy that the goldfish uses. When the energy is totally used up, the goldfish should die. However, the goldfish keeps moving around for two months, three months, or even as long as five months. It means that the energy must come from outside the container.

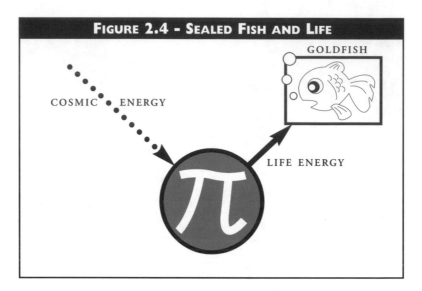

COSMIC ENERGY WAS FOOD FOR THE GOLDFISH

Let's think about the cosmic energy that is all around us just like electric waves. Cosmic energy's wave length is such that living creatures cannot use it as it is. In order for living things to utilize cosmic energy, it is necessary to change its wave length so that it is more suitable for them. If Pi-Water is doing that job, then Pi-Water would continue to radiate living energy forever. Thus, a goldfish could keep on living for several months. We think that Pi-Water plays the role of changing cosmic energy to living energy. (See Figure 2.4: Sealed Fish and Life.) In this case, we designated cosmic energy as the energy source, but it is not necessary to limit the source to cosmic energy alone. What other kinds of energy are there?

Just as a goldfish in a sealed container filled with Pi-Water can continue to live by using cosmic energy, human beings can use cosmic energy as well. As an example, the monks of Mt. Hiei, through their strict training, have proven this.

CONTRADICTION BETWEEN THE TRAINING OF
MT. HIEI MONKS AND NUTRITION

The monks endure strict training at Mt. Hiei; the most difficult training exercise of all is called one-thousand-day training, during

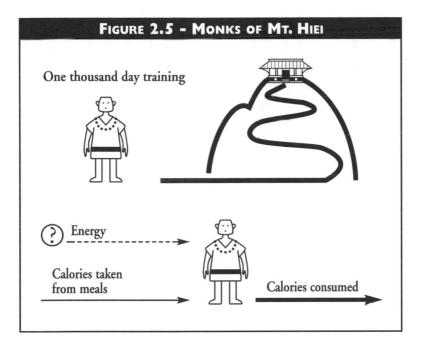

FIGURE 2.5 - MONKS OF MT. HIEI

One thousand day training

? Energy

Calories taken from meals

Calories consumed

which they walk 30 kilometers of mountain paths every day. Although the exercise specifies one thousand days, it actually takes not just over three years, but as long as seven years, because the monks engage in various kinds of training procedures, such as staying under a waterfall on the way or climbing down the mountain on one occasion.

The monks eat a limited vegetarian meal during this rigid training, consisting of one helping of soup and one helping of vegetables. They use up several thousand calories a day, while taking in only several hundred calories a day from their meals. (See Figure 2.5: Monks of Mt. Hiei.) Modern nutrition cannot explain how they can survive, as their intake and output of calories differ by one digit. It is called "the mystery of nutrition." Let us presume that the training monks use cosmic energy as the energy source besides foods.

Cosmic energy cannot be used by living things directly, as mentioned earlier, but what is wonderful about human beings is that we have the capability to be able to use it. With years of training, humans come closer to spiritual awakening, and the waves of energy from the living body become higher. Thus, humans are able to use the same waves of cosmic energy. In fact, the monks of Mt. Hiei must go through five years of training prior to this one-thousand-day training. Only those who achieve spiritual awakening are allowed to begin the training. This means that if they come to their spiritual awakening, they are able to live without food. They may have known about this unseen energy from ancient times.

In India there is an even more cruel training program for higher level monks. Trainers place a monk who has come to a spiritual awakening in a wooden box and bury it underground four meters below the surface. When they dig up the box six months later, the monk is alive and quite healthy, although he never ate or drank during this period. This is exactly the same phenomenon as the goldfish in a sealed container.

HOW TO IDENTIFY PI-WATER

There are mainly two ways to make Pi-Water. One way is to dissolve a small amount of ferric/ferrous ($Fe^{II/III}$) in water, and the other way is to use a medium.

As a medium, Pi-ceramic or Pi-air is generally used. When water comes in contact with the medium, water receives Pi (aura) energy and becomes Pi-Water. The basic ingredient of Pi-Water is ferric/ferrous salt, but it does not necessarily have to be the water containing ferric/ferrous salt. It is the water retaining ferric/ferrous salt information.

The most accurate method that we confirmed to detect Pi-Water is through bio-assay, or living creatures inspection method. In this method, we do not measure physical values but observe and confirm actual influences on living creatures. For example:

1. Soak seeds of green beans in Pi-Water for 30 minutes. Take them out and rinse them thoroughly with water.
2. After draining excess water from the beans, place them on moist vermiculite.
3. Place in a plastic wrap, and keep them in a dark homoiothermal container at 25–30°C. Make a comparison experi-

ment with seeds not treated with Pi-Water and grow them at the same time.

4. Five to seven days later, when the stems become 10–15 cm long, remove the beans from the vermiculite and count the number of roots. There are obviously more roots on the seeds treated with Pi-Water compared to those not treated.

You don't have to use green bean seeds for this experiment. Other kinds of seeds may be used.

Other methods of identifying Pi-Water are copper-nitric acid reaction, dowsing, and the O-ring test. Unfortunately, they only prove one aspect of Pi-Water, or they have problems with reproduction, and thus they are not very accurate. This is because the essence of Pi-Water is aura energy, which is a kind of electromagnetic wave. So, unless you can measure both wave length and the rate of strength, you cannot have an accurate measurement. You may understand this more easily if you think of the energy of light.

It is important to remember that strong energy is not always the best. Energy with good wave length could be harmful if it is too strong. We need to choose the wave length and energy strength appropriate to the object that we are studying.

COPPER-NITRIC ACID REACTION METHOD
When you add concentrated nitric acid to copper powders dissolved in water, the solution turns blue as copper nitrate is formed. However, Pi-Water does not change color because it suppresses this oxidizing reaction.

DOWSING
Put a weight on a piece of string about 15 cm long and make a judgment from the rotation of this weight. The weight should ideally be Pi-ceramic or a magnet, but if they are not available, any solid object should work.

Hold the string between your fingers and let the weight stay still above Pi-Water. After a while, it will start to rotate either clockwise or counterclockwise. The direction of the rotation depends on the individual person, so you need to confirm which is the correct rotation. For example, good things rotate counter-clockwise and bad things rotate clockwise.

O-RING TEST

A subject holds Pi-Water in his left hand and make an O with the index finger and thumb of his or her right hand. Another person puts both of his index fingers in the O-ring and pulls to the left and right. The test is to compare the rate of strength of this O-ring when the other person tries to pull it apart. This test is used at several university hospitals during examinations. If you do this correctly, you will have a high rate of success. For example, the difference between the strength the subject has when holding a magnetic card in his or her left hand and when not is quite obvious to everyone. When you do this O-ring test with the subject holding something harmful to his health such as cigarette, the O-ring can be opened easily. When the subject is holding something good for health, the O-ring does not open so easily.

CHAPTER THREE

DISEASES AND BIO-ENERGY

WHY MORE DISEASES EXIST DESPITE ADVANCED MEDICINE

Japanese people have worked really hard, believing that their lives would improve when they could catch up with Europe and America and restore the society completely ruined by World War II. Thanks to this exceptional vitality of the people, Japan has become a leader in the industrial world, manufacturing good quality electric appliances, automobiles, cameras, watches, and other products. However, in doing so, we ruined our environment. In order to achieve mass production and mass consumption, it is necessary to eliminate as much as possible the trouble of manually making products. Therefore, a large amount of chemicals have been used, and production processes have been automated. In order to comply with the needs of a society of mass consumption, we have used food additives and agricultural chemicals. The result is that our health has been seriously affected.

According to data (See Graph 3.1: Patients with Major Illnesses.) presented in a white paper issued by the Ministry of Welfare in 1987, there has been a rapid increase of cancer, liver disorders, heart diseases, apoplexy, mental illnesses, and disorders caused by high blood pressure.

In 1960 tuberculosis outnumbered all the other diseases. There were not many antibiotics around and people normally did not recover once they contracted the disease. With the advance of modern medicine, antibiotics that fight bacteria and vaccinations against viruses have been developed. Tuberculosis patients decreased year by year, and now there are only very few. Lethal infectious diseases such as cholera and typhoid have disappeared with the construction of sewer systems. Travelers get infected with these diseases occasionally, but it does not present any problems because we now have vaccines to prevent and combat diseases. Nonetheless, how can we explain the fact that the number of patients is increasing despite more advanced medicine?

THREE OUT OF FOUR DIE OF CANCER

With the Westernization of Japanese diets, there has been a big increase of so-called degenerative diseases, such as high blood

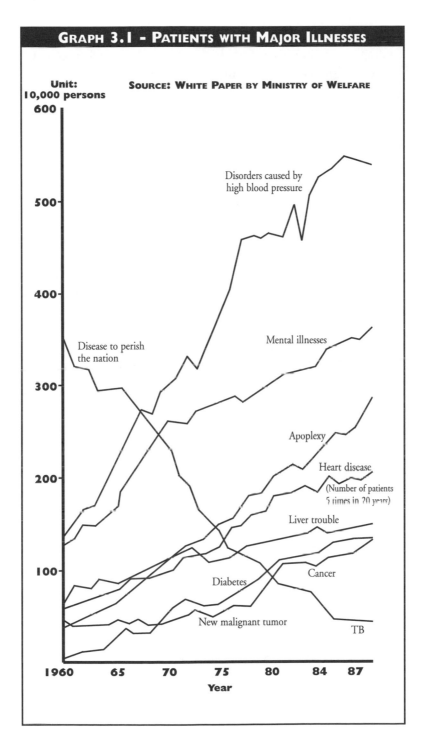

GRAPH 3.1 - PATIENTS WITH MAJOR ILLNESSES

Unit:
10,000 persons

SOURCE: WHITE PAPER BY MINISTRY OF WELFARE

Disorders caused by
high blood pressure

Mental illnesses

Disease to perish
the nation

Apoplexy

Heart disease

(Number of patients
5 times in 20 years)

Liver trouble

Diabetes

Cancer

New malignant tumor

TB

Year

pressure, apoplexy, heart disease, and diabetes. Around 1975 the leading cause of death was cerebral vein troubles, such as cerebral infarction and cerebral thrombosis, but now the primary causes of death are heart disease and cancer. One out of four people die of cancer; you may know of persons around you who are suffering from cancer.

Please note that we need to be careful about these numbers, which are just statistical figures. There is an important hidden fact behind them.

The "complete cure" is based on the rate of patients who lived for five years after their recovery. So, if there is no trouble for five years after they recover, according to the statistics, they are deemed to recovered completely. However, there are many who die after five years, in some cases in the sixth year of recovery, as cancer starts to spread to other organs.

For example, a patient recovers from stomach cancer, lives at home for five years. There isn't any sign or symptom noted during these five years. In the sixth year, however, he gets sick, has a checkup, and finds that cancer has spread into his pancreas. In this case, he now has pancreas cancer. With the treatment, he again has no symptoms for the next five years. Then he dies as cancer spreads to his brain. According to the statistics, he has attained 60 percent recovery.

The rate of having cancer is higher for older people. However, their cancer grows slowly. For example, although a patient has cancer at the age of 70, by the time he dies, he has so many other disorders that his death may be regarded as having occurred as a result of other diseases.

If we analyze the data more thoroughly, we find that the death rate of cancer suffering patients would not be one out of four, but one out of two. Or if we include the patients who died of other diseases triggered by cancer, it would be more like three out of four.

MORE INFLUENCE OF AGRICULTURAL CHEMICALS

Hokkaido has the image of having rich natural treasures. We tend to buy products from Hokkaido, such as milk and crops, assuming that they are free from chemicals. Many of us think that those who are engaged in agriculture or diary farming in Hokkaido must lead healthy lives.

The area around Lake Mashu gets extremely cold, which presents a difficult problem for farming. In addition, this area has been increasingly losing its labor force because many young people do not want to work as farmers, and they leave this area. As a result, fewer farmers work in larger fields, compared to Honshu. The size of the area that one farmer has to work on is three times as big as it used to be. This problem is not just in Hokkaido.

In order to work on the same sized fields with fewer hands, farmers need to spray weed killer and other agricultural chemicals, trying to achieve efficiency. The agricultural chemicals really affect the people who live there. There is a horrible estimation that one out of three people may develop cancer. Everyone knows that agricultural chemicals are dangerous. However, they have not yet found effective and safe alternatives.

PREGNANT, BUT CANNOT GIVE BIRTH TO HEALTHY BABIES

When women become pregnant, they submit a pregnancy report and receive a "Mother and Child Booklet." Let's refer to the number of women who receive the booklet as A and the number of women who delivered their babies and submitted a report on the birth of a child as B. A minus B would be the number of fetuses that died. Graph 3.2: Change in Miscarriage Rate (Tokyo) illustrates the comparison of that number. It shows that in 1987 9.5 percent of the women who became pregnant did not deliver live babies for some reason. In 1955, the figure was 8.33 percent. The Morinaga arsenic poisoned milk incident occurred that year. You can see a considerable difference from the year after. About 2 percent may be the figure that is generally considered as the minimum rate of miscarriage. Then what happened to the other 6 percent, as we subtract two from eight? How and why did those women miscarry their fetuses?

The number of miscarriages has been increasing since 1960. This was the same era when consumption of artificial sweetener, kanemi oil, AF2, and other food additives increased quite rapid-

GRAPH 3.2 - CHANGE OF MISCARRIAGE RATE (TOKYO)

VITAL STATISTICS BY THE MINISTRY OF PUBLIC WELFARE

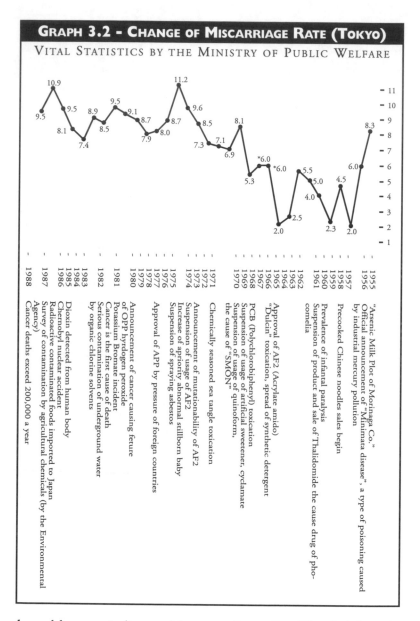

ly and became indispensable parts of our diet. The thalidomide incident and Dulcin poisoning occurred. Instant ramen noodles appeared on the market in 1958. There was then a rapid increase among newborn babies who were affected by poisonous substances, such as PCB, which their mothers had taken.

Currently, there are numerous kinds of food additives. The Hygiene Agency of the Ministry of Welfare announced that the average food additives intake per day of an an adult is about 100 mg.

With various kinds of instant foods, retort foods, and soft drinks readily available from vending machines, it has become possible for us to eat or drink any time anywhere. The consumer demand for this kind of lifestyle was the power that pushed the Japanese GNP to number one in the world. However, now we are paying for this kind of lifestyle by placing our health at risk. Our present health disorders are caused by additives and chemicals because we chose this lifestyle over previous natural ways.

By 1970 we were enjoying our freedom and materialistically abundant life with the Japan Reconstruction Plan. But on the other hand, such dangerous things as we explained above were going on, generating the condition in which women could not have babies as they wanted to. Even if they were lucky enough to be able to deliver babies, there was an increasing number of fetuses that showed abnormalities affected by chemicals that cause abnormal chromosomes and lead to congenital diseases. Eczema is one of the ailments.

Some children have even become paralyzed on one side or have a high blood fat content. The number of children who suffer from incurable diseases such as collagen disease or chronic maladies is increasing. It is easy to blame the parents, but we should be able to figure out what we must do, considering the social background.

We have let changes in the environment take over the natural order. We have also let Western medicine, which regards the body only as a collective entity consisting of independent parts, dominate. When we reflect on what we have done, we realize that we have left behind the important cosmic law, which is to live in harmony with nature. Having neglected that law, we now face such problems.

The 21st century is just around the corner. Japanese are rare people who are able to understand both Western and Eastern ways of thinking. What we need to do now is to normalize our environment and create healthy and bright societies at the same time. To do so we need to raise the consciousness of the people.

THE CAUSE OF ALL DISEASES IS LACK OF ENERGY

We get sick because our energy level decreases. Human beings possess the strongest armor against diseases—natural healing power. But if life energy goes down, we lose this natural healing power. Life energy is equivalent to *ki* in Oriental medicine. Life energy, *ki,* controls the cerebrum's functions, such as the hypothalamus and central nerves, and normalizes functions that are off balance. This activates the natural healing power that human beings are born with. That is why people get sick naturally if life energy goes down and recover if energy is supplemented.

This *ki,* life energy, has a network linking 365 spots on the surface of a human body. This link even goes to the internal organs. The spots linked to internal organs are concentrated on the back of the feet, palms, and ears. When you have a stomach upset, for example, you can find out how to get better by pressing certain spots on the back of your feet. By stimulating these spots, you supplement energy to this link, thus activating the flow of life energy.

Since there is no scientific basis to the concept that diseases are cured with life energy, many doctors of Western medicine are skeptical. This is quite natural as Western and Oriental medicine have very different approaches to the body. Western medicine is based on the materialistic way of thinking and regards the human body as consisting of different parts. So, you can just remove the bad parts and kill viruses with antibiotics. You only need to know the cause of the disease. We do owe much to the development of Western medicine for what we are today. With vaccination and antibiotics, most simple diseases were cured. However, we do not know the causes of the incurable diseases, degenerative diseases, and diseases of the aged. Western medicine has not yet discovered how to solve these problems. There is a big wall standing in front of the Western medicine now.

On the other hand, Oriental medicine based on life energy is quite effective for diseases with unknown causes. Its immediate effect has also been proven when China disclosed the documentary film showing surgeries in which only acupuncture was used for anesthesia, which totally shocked the Western medicine world.

The reason that this life energy was named *ki* is that the Chinese realized human beings are controlled by this mysterious power that is far more powerful than their own, and that this power is the source of life. To do anything against the natural way is to go against cosmic rules, which destroys the balance between nature and people, affecting everything else. It is amazing that this principle was understood in China 2,000 years before Christ was born.

RAISING *KI* MEANS RAISING CONSCIOUSNESS

The *kiko* method by which one takes *ki* into the body is the best way to draw in cosmic energy from the natural air. The most important thing in *kiko* is the breathing method. Originally, the *kiko* method existed for people to raise their consciousness to the highest level. In *kiko's* thinking, *ki* means energy, therefore it was regarded as a health improvement method.

Human consciousness is extremely important, above anything else, and it is also a form of energy. If you think you are sick, then you are bound to get sick. If you sincerely pray so that your work will be successful, it will. So, it is important to raise your consciousness while you are healthy.

Let us assume there is a person who has very low consciousness and who is always negative. If he gets sick, no matter how hard you try to treat him, or even if he used Pi-Water as the last resort, he would not get well unless his consciousness was raised. The energy of your consciousness is that powerful. You must raise your own consciousness at the same time as drawing living energy from outside. When you get sick, it is important for you to keep trying to live with the firm belief that you will recover.

LIFE IS ENERGY

When we talk about what life is, in most cases we mean the difference between being alive and being dead. Recently, brain death has aroused controversy and made it apparent that everyone has his or her own interpretation of death. If someone's heart stops beating, then everyone thinks that person has died. As far as this phenomenon is concerned, death seems clear. But, if asked what color or shape life is, you may find it difficult to answer. Life does not have any color or shape, because life is energy itself. When energy is insufficient, you get sick. When it is supplemented or replaced, you recover. Human beings are a mass of energy or energy itself.

However, we call energy something we can see and feel, such as thermal energy, electrical energy, and gravitational energy. We need to realize that we are already controlled by the energy that we cannot see. This is called life energy, consciousness energy, or aura energy, and although it cannot be measured by modern science, it can influence our bodies. Take an ulcer, for example. Modern medicine regards a body as a substance and the stomach only as a part. If you think of an ulcer in a materialistic way, then you cannot solve the problem, and other parts of your body will be affected by medicine. To prove that a human being is not a collection of materials, you can subject a person to extreme stress, and his stomach will soon develop a hole.

Long ago there was a private school named Totsuka Yacht School. The instructors trained their students in a very severe, strict manner. One of the students died in an accident, and this school was presented with a serious social problem. An autopsy of this student revealed that his stomach had a large hole. The students received what was called special training during which instructors pushed them into the ocean and beat them, causing severe stress among the students.

When a follow-up survey was conducted on those who were born in Germany during the World War II, there was high rate of homosexuality among them. Their mothers were under extreme stress during the war, which affected their fetuses. Even though the fetus was not aware, its mother's consciousness affected it.

When you become sick, your own and other people's consciousness makes you sick. When you think, "Many people in my family have got cancer, so I probably will have cancer," you may actually develop cancer. Or, if you get cancer and say, "I lost a lot of weight because of cancer," or "Diet is really important for cancer," then everyone around you will know and become conscious that you do have cancer, so that you will be surrounded by those with negative consciousness stating you will never recover even if you have a chance. The energy of your consciousness is really powerful.

THE HUNDREDTH MONKEY

On an isolated small island on the east coast of Kyushu, a group of 100 monkeys lived in a natural setting. One day one of them happened to wash a sweet potato in the sea water and discovered that it tasted better with salt. Other monkeys imitated the first monkey and started to do the same thing. Finally all 100 of them were eating sweet potatoes after washing them in the sea water.

Then, suddenly a group of monkeys that lived on an island 10 to 20 km away started to wash their food in sea water before eating. This habit spread like a chain reaction to the monkeys living on islands far away until finally the monkeys on Takasaki Mountain in Honshu, several hundred kilometers away, began to eat like this. The consciousness of these first 100 monkeys on the isolated island influenced those several hundred kilometers away.

This story originally appeared in the book entitled *Life Tide*, written by Rial Watson, in the chapter entitled "When the 100th monkey appears." This story shows that when consciousness gathers, it turns into energy that can affect others. Therefore, we human beings need to raise our consciousness to the highest possible level.

Environmental destruction, water pollution—it all happens because our consciousness makes it happen. The more careful people become not to pollute water and the environment, then the more likely environmental pollution will end. If you think, "One person cannot make a significant difference," then your consciousness is making a step toward destruction of the environment. We have pursued convenience, leaving the most important consciousness elsewhere.

THE AIDS VIRUS DOES NOT PROLIFERATE UNDER
HIGH ENERGY

AIDS (Acquired Immune Deficiency Syndrome) has become one of the most serious worldwide problems in this century. We have not yet found any special remedy for the AIDS virus. Although scientists and companies have been trying to develop anti-AIDS medicines, they have had difficulty finding an effective vaccination.

An AIDS institute in an American university performed an interesting experiment, trying to see if Pi-Water could exterminate the AIDS virus. The result was that when the AIDS virus was cultivated within a Pi-Water environment, it started to die, whereas normal cells kept multiplying. Pi-Water gives energy to normal cells so that they can grow in the right way, as they were originally meant to do. The AIDS virus, which is a bad influence, cannot survive the high energy of Pi-Water. The study is not yet completed. However, when the time comes, all the results will be out in the open, and scientists will be able to develop and market appropriate products.

RELIGION IS SCIENCE

Long ago religion used to be considered science itself. People today have an image of religion as being nonscientific or remote from science.

In the long human history of thousands of years, religion and science have been separated from each other only for the past 200 years or so. Before that religion used to be science itself. Religion certainly had some ill effects. We all know that Galileo, who advocated the Copernican system stating the planets revolve around the sun, said, "But the earth is still turning," at his religious trial in the 17th century. This is a famous story. However, we cannot conclude religion itself is not scientific, since religion has been around for thousands of years.

Modern science is based on positivism, and it regards "being able to prove" as the premise of science. But we have been influenced too much by this, and we tend to think that what we cannot understand or prove is not scientific. This may be a big mistake. Whatever modern science has disclosed is only a speck in the cosmos. The Bible tells us stories of Jesus Christ healing the sick just by putting his hands over them. Are these descriptions in the New Testament merely parables?

If you think of Jesus' healing the sick from a scientific point of view, he cured the illnesses because he gave his strong living energy to the sick. Sickness, without a single exception, is caused by a lack of living energy. People may say, "That cannot be. AIDS is caused by a virus, and tuberculosis is caused by tubercle bacillus bacteria." But some people catch cold and some do not even if they are in the same environment. The difference lies in whether they are filled with living energy or they lack it. Those who are filled with living energy will not contract a cold virus. Only those who lack living energy would pick up a virus and catch cold as the result.

As mentioned before, living energy is aura energy itself. The living energy that Jesus used was aura energy.

Recently in Japan, the effect of the *kiko* treatment has drawn much attention. *Ki* in *kiko* is the same as aura energy. It just has a different name. *Kiko* has been practiced in China for 4,000 years. There is no mystery to it. Therefore, Jesus Christ did something quite rational, and what is written in the Bible is consistent with Eastern scientific reasoning.

EINSTEIN SCIENTIFICALLY PROVED PRAJNA-PARAMITA-SUTRA

The shortest sacred book in the world is *Prajna-paramita-sutra*, which consists of 267 letters. It has been passed from generation to generation for thousands of years. The most important phrase consists of eight letters, "色即是空. 空即是色." The eight letters mean "All is vanity, vanity is all." We need to understand how these letters are interpreted.

Generally, the character "色" means "material world" or "world of phenomena," thus "this world we live in." The more difficult character is "空" for emptiness. It is even said that if you understand the meaning of this "空", then you are able to understand the entire *Prajna-paramit-sutra* "空" is interpreted as "emptiness" or "vain," so naturally the meaning of these letters is interpreted as "this world is vain." And your destination is the world of "all phenomena are transitory."

Indeed, many think "空" means energy. Energy does not have color or shape, and we cannot touch it. Because the authors did not understand the concept of energy at the time when this sacred book was written, they had to express that concept as "空". At any rate, if "空" means energy, then these eight letters can be interpreted as "material is energy, energy is material." Let's recall the equation of Einstein's specific theory of relativity:

$$E = MC^2$$

E is energy, M is mass, and C is the speed of light. So the above equation means "energy is the mass of the material multiplied by the square of the speed of light." This means the same as "energy is material, material is energy." Therefore, this means that the specific theory of relativity expresses the same concept as *Prajna-paramita-sutra*. So, it was Einstein who scientifically proved *Prajna-paramita-sutra*.

If *Prajna-paramita-sutra* was the specific theory of relativity itself, then it was naturally a book of religion, philosophy, and science.

CHAPTER FOUR

❈ ❈ ❈

AMAZING CLINICAL DATA
WITH PI-WATER

CHALLENGING SOME INCURABLE DISEASES
WITH THE PI-WATER

There are many people who say, "With Pi-Water, my disease that caused many years of suffering was cured." Whenever I meet someone suffering from a disease, I recommended Pi-Water. Have them drink Pi-Water—it is just a little help from an amateur. Many readers may not be able to believe me when I talk about the cases of diseases being cured. I do not blame their thinking because I am not a medical doctor. Some people may think, "Nothing can be so effective and work so quickly. It must be the same sort of health improving method I see all the time in health magazines." These people are so strongly influenced by the phenomenal science that they have been taught at school. They have acquired a habit of not believing what science cannot prove, even if they can actually see it with their eyes.

However, there are multitude of phenomena that we cannot prove or explain. In fact, we can prove very few things with science. For example, in Western medicine, we cannot even understand the mechanism of how we get sick or how diseases occur. It

TABLE 4.1 - HIGH ENERGY PI-WATER TREATMENT (34 OUTPATIENTS)					
ITEMS / NAME OF ILLNESS	NO. OF PATIENTS PI-WATER IS GIVEN	CONDITIONS OF GIVING PI-WATER			
		NO. OF TIMES/DAY	NO. OF DROPS/ ONE TIME IN 200ML	NO. OF DROPS/DAY	DURATION IN MONTHS
Arthritis (other)	25	2-5	3	6-9	3
Cirrhosis	1	3-4	3	9-12	3
Liver Cancer	1	10	10	100	3
Rectal Cancer (terminal)	1	10	10	100	3
Erythematosus	1	10	3	30	12
Diabetes	2	5	5	25	3
Diabetes	3	5	3	15	4

* for drinking water, we used the Pi-Water purifier.

is the same way with *kiko*. It is absolutely impossible to explain *kiko* scientifically with present-day science.

Among the amazing effects of Pi-Water is its use to improve human beings' health. Clinical experiments have proven its effectiveness in various fields of medicine.

IMPROVEMENT EFFECT OBSERVATION DATA

To illustrate my experiments with Pi-Water, I organized my clinical data from a hospital in Hokkaido where I used to work. The duration of the study was three months, and there were 34 patients. (See Table 4.1: High Energy Pi-Water Treatment (34 Outpatients.) The patients had such diseases as arthritis, lower back pain, trigominal nerve pain, difficulty in walking, inability to work, limited shoulder movement, fatigue, chills, insomnia, constipation, hemorrhoids, blood sugar disorders, psychosomatic illnesses, dizziness, speech disorders, urination problems, abdominal disorders, aerophasia, neurosis, angina pectoris, diarrhea, asthma, and menopausal discomfort. (See Table 4.2: Improvement Seen by Giving Hi-energy Pi-Water and Side Effects.) The number of diseases is inconsistent because we took data from the patients who came to the hospital during a short period of time.

The data are based on the observation of improvement of the patients' symptoms while deciding the amount of Pi-Water to be given according to their symptoms and actually giving it to respective patients. There was no report on side effects, and its effect was significant.

As shown in Table 4.2, out of 15 patients suffering from arthritis, 14 were seriously ill, and one was in middle degree. Twelve of them improved from seriously ill to slightly ill, two of them from seriously ill to completely free from symptoms. The one who had middle degree arthritis improved to only slightly ill. For 14 patients, it was extremely effective, and for one patient it was effective.

TABLE 4.2 – IMPROVEMENT SEEN BY GIVING HIGH-ENERGY PI-WATER AND SIDE EFFECTS

SYMPTOM	NUMBER	SERIOUS-SLIGHT	SERIOUS-FREE	MEDIUM-SLIGHT	VERY EFFECTIVE	EFFECTIVE	S:???
Lsychosomatic	1	1			1	1	None
Dizziness	1	1			1		None
Speech disorder	1	1			1		None
Urination disorder	1	1			1		None
Abdomen discomfort	3	3			3		None
Carefree	1	1			1		None
Neurosis	1					1	None
Angina pectoris	1	1		1	1		None
Diarrhea	1		1		1		None
Asthma	2	2			2		None
Menopause	1	1			1		None
Arthritis	15	12	2	1	14	1	None
Lower back pain	5	4		1	4	1	None
Neuralgia	4	3	1		4		None
Walking difficulty	7	6		1	6	1	None
Unable to work	7	7			7		None
Limit to shoulder movement (2 cases of calcification)	4	2	2		4		None
Fatigue	2	2	2		2		None
Chilling (serious)	4	4			4		None
Insomnia (serious)	5	5			5		None
Constipation	3	3			3		None
Hemorrhoids	2	2	2		2		None
Blood sugar	5	5			5		None

CLINICAL SUCCESS CASES AS REPORTED
BY PHYSICIANS

Case Reports by Dr. Takafumi Tsurumi
(Tsurumi Clinic, Shizuoka Prefecture)

COMMENTS BY DR. TSURUMI—CANCER PATIENT WHO HAS
BEEN
GIVEN UP BY A LARGE HOSPITAL

Ms. K came to our clinic on March 3, 1993. She said that six years ago she was in a large hospital in Hamamatsu city, where she underwent an evaluation of what had been diagnosed as a gastric ulcer. In fact, rather than an ulcer, she had gastric cancer that required removal of about 80 percent of her stomach. She had never been told the real diagnosis by her physician.

She continued to suffer from mild fever (37.3°C) for about a year following the surgery. The hospital staff determined that the cancer she had in her stomach had spread to her lymphatic system. However, four years went by and she was not getting particularly worse. Then she was found to have an ileus (obstruction) of her transverse colon, for which she had surgery at the nearby hospital. Again she was not told the real diagnosis by her physicians although they could see a cancer very clearly that was certainly distinguishable from an ulcer.

In July 1992 she was rushed to the hospital again with a recurrent ileus. Since then, she has suffered various symptoms such as poor appetite and fatigue. When they checked her colon, they could see it was definitely cancer. Another new cancer appeared in her body—colon cancer.

By the end of February 1993, she had developed an ileus for the third time. Her family was told that her colon cancer had spread into the pancreas and small intestine. She had to have surgery immediately. At the same hospital, she was scheduled for surgery on March 6.

When she first came to our clinic, she appeared ill and physically and mentally weak. Her skin was very dry from dehydration. She was depressed and had almost given up the idea of recovery.

She did not have jaundice or anemia; however, there was a palpable mass on the abdomen that seemed to be cancer.

After having many surgeries, she became completely exhausted. I could sense that if she had another surgical operation in the hospital, she would not live. I also believed that she could not recover unless she was informed that she had cancer. So I asked her family to tell her truth. I told them that there might be good chance of a recovery and even a cure. I asked them to leave the patient entirely in my care.

When she was told that she had cancer, she felt better. She even said, "I was relieved to be told the truth." I spoke with her for a couple of hours about various approaches of treatment and the fact that she did not even have to be hospitalized.

From that time, I had her drink high energy Pi-Water as part of the treatment regimen. Although she was scheduled to have an operation on March 6, her check-up revealed no more obstructions. Thus, it was not necessary for her to have surgery. She no longer felt nauseated, and she started to have normal bowel movements immediately. She made a very rapid recovery. I was convinced that the cancer could be cured completely.

Her recent blood biochemistry data revealed normal values. She was very well and free from any apparent symptoms, such as nausea, constipation and abdominal pain. If you have cancer in the large intestine, an immunological blood test of the stool tends to be positive, but in her case it was negative. Eventually, with a biopsy, we will be able to tell whether she has recovered or not. However, I don't see the necessity to do a biopsy or an analysis with a colonoscope now that she has recovered. Quality of life is important. For this patient, everything has been cleared up. However, she still has cancer in one part of her large intestine, but I am certain that it will disappear in a short while. It takes three years for all the human cells to replace themselves. Her cells are in the middle of that cycle. Angiography, MRI, CT, and barium X-ray all showed that her cancer had not spread. The remaining cancer is shrinking little by little.

Ms. K, age 57 — "The days of suffering
seem like a dream..."

It was in the beginning of March 1993 when I was told that I had cancer in my colon. The doctor told me that the cancer had become larger and had spread to the pancreas and small intestine. The suffering and pain I was going through at that time were beyond description because cancer had spread all through my digestive organs.

I had surgery six years ago and had about 80 percent of my stomach removed. They told me it was a gastric ulcer. This was the beginning. I did not recover very well after the first surgery. Then I had an ulcer in the intestine and had a part of that removed two years ago. Once again, I did not recover and had bad pains and ileus in the intestine.

In July 1992 I was hospitalized for one month with a severe ileus and terrible pain then discharged with little improvement. But I still did not feel better afterward. However, according to all the laboratory examinations, there was nothing abnormal. I continued to struggle with pain for several months. On February 27, 1993, I got very sick again and a laboratory examination was done. The doctor told my family, but not me, that I had cancer in the intestine. In addition, the cancer in my pancreas and small intestine had become larger. The doctor said that surgery was necessary and that it would be difficult because he would also have to remove my pancreas and small intestine.

One day before surgery, an acquaintance of mine referred me to Dr. Tsurumi, who confirmed I had cancer. I thought, "Maybe I cannot recover." However, while talking with him, I felt there was hope for recovery. If I had not consulted Dr. Tsurumi, I would not be alive today.

After I consulted with Dr. Tsurumi, I started drinking high energy Pi-Water. I have continued with his treatment, trusting him completely.

In the beginning, since I am not good at getting up in the morning, I was not sure if I could really make it to his clinic. I tried to encourage myself, thinking that I must be tough. I drive from

Hamamatsu by myself to come to his clinic. Since I have begun drinking Pi-Water, I feel incredibly strong by the time I go home.

It has been three and half months since I started Dr. Tsurumi's treatment. Now I no longer have any pain or symptoms of ileus. I eat normally and regularly, leading the life of a healthy person. It's unbelievable how I have recovered. At this moment, I am not working, but I am full of energy and feel like going back to work right now.

COMMENTS BY DR. TSURUMI — "THE BLADDER ALMOST HAD TO BE EXTRACTED..."

Mr. F is 75 years old. He had bloody urine five years ago and was hospitalized. Surgery was done to remove 25 percent of his urinary bladder since he had cancer there. He started having bloody urine again about two years ago, but he did not think it was a serious problem and didn't do anything about it.

In February 1993 blood in his urine became a really serious problem. He was hospitalized for a month in the next town. During this hospitalization no treatment was given to him. He had a series of examinations that indicated he needed to have another operation. He got out of the hospital and came to my clinic on February 25.

He came to see me hoping that there might be a way to recover without having surgery. I was convinced that he must absolutely avoid an extensive surgery, such as purification of the bladder or lymph nodes, because of his age. Since I am not a urologist, I could not do a biopsy. However, biopsy was done in the hospital and his cell exam showed Class 5 (there are Classes 1 through 5), which meant that he definitely had cancer. Since he was losing a lot of blood in his urine, he was also a little anemic. His doctor had never told him that he had cancer. He seemed to be very calm when I told him. I thought he was a very calm person. I started giving him Pi-Water and a blood transfusion at the same time since he was passing so much blood in his urine.

On May 24, 1993, biopsy was done again, and his cell exam showed Class 4. There were very small numbers of cancer cells. I gradually decreased the number of blood transfusions.

Since his urinary bladder cancer was cured, the cell exam result went up. I was hoping that he would recover completely before the cancer would spread. The biochemistry exams conducted in 1994 showed that everything was back to normal.

MR. F, AGE 75—"SAVED BY DR. TSURUMI"

About five years ago, I was surprised to find that I was passing blood in my urine. I rushed to the nearby hospital to have an examination. They told me that I had some kind of bacterial infection, and that I may develop cancer if I did not do anything about it. I had surgery there and had 25 percent of the edge of my bladder removed. I was not informed that it was cancer.

I continued to have checkups for about two years. Then I stopped going to the hospital because I thought that I would be OK. However, blood started passing out again every now and then. At the end of 1992, I passed a lot of blood, but it stopped. I got concerned and went to another hospital a little further away and was examined and admitted there. They told me that I had to have all of my bladder removed. When my sister heard that, she got in touch with Dr. Tsurumi. So I met him and talked with him. I had never met any doctor like Dr. Tsurumi, who would talk to a patient with a complete understanding as to how we patients feel. I was really pleased to meet him. He told me that I did not have to worry since I can recover without surgery.

When I first visited his clinic, I felt weak and heavy because of anemia. However, there was no pain. After having an IVF drip infusion treatment and my bladder cleaned, the color of my urine turned pink. I began to feel that maybe I could recover.

I was given high energy Pi-Water from Dr. Tsurumi and drank 10 drops at a time, three times a day, every day. He wanted me to increase the amount, so I did. Later I had a week when the color of my urine continued to be transparent which made me think that I was cured. However, it turned pink again and became transparent again. I felt that I was certainly on the way toward recovery.

Sometimes, I pass out blood clots as big as raisins. Right after I got out of the hospital, I used to have them clog my ureter since I was not able to pass any urine. When I think back, a feeling tells me that I have made a tremendous recovery. It has been only three months since I got out of the hospital in February.

COMMENTS BY DR. TSURUMI — "EXTREMELY EFFECTIVE FOR LIVER..."

This patient was diagnosed as having diabetes, hypertension, chronic hepatitis, liver cirrhosis secondary to chronic hepatitis, and liver cancer. He knows he has cancer, but he does not seem to be concerned about it very much.

There are different kinds of hepatitis, depending on the infection routes. Type C is the infection contracted through the abuse of drugs such as methamphetamine and stimulant drugs or through blood transfusions. Delivery is an infection route for Type B, as it is a vertical infection route. It would be very rare that a Type C virus completely dies. However if you have it under control, you can live to your life expectancy. You must be careful though. If you do not take care of it even for a short period of time, it can turn rapidly into cirrhosis or liver cancer.

The number of people infected by Type C hepatitis is increasing these days. Interferon is said to be a special remedy for Type C cirrhosis, but I personally do not like this medicine and doubt if it really is effective. There have been many articles recently about the side effects of interferon. At our clinic, many of my patients do not want to use interferon.

I use a lot of high energy Pi-Water, but I don't think the Type C hepatitis HCV antibody would completely disappear. Using interferon does not make the HCV antibody disappear either. In view of interferon's bad side effects and the fact that its positive effects seem unclear, I believe Pi-Water is so much better and more effective.

The most important thing is that a patient can lead a normal life with high consciousness without suffering from symptoms for a long time. However, in reality, many patients suffer every day as their daily activities are limited and they endure painful treatment. My role is to help patients obtain a better quality of life and to enjoy their lives even up to 90 or 100 years of age.

With Mr. T, he has a history of alcohol and methamphetamine abuse when he was young and his bad eating habits combined to worsen his condition. He was rushed to our clinic because he was very close to going into a ketoacidosis coma from his diabetes.

I used an IVF drip infusion and high energy Pi-Water. I directed him to improve his eating habits and gave him *ki* treatment and healing procedures. As the result, he recovered from diabetes quickly , but still suffered from Type C hepatitis. However, all the elements of Type C hepatitis, such as transaminase, GOT, and GPT were quite satisfactory, and he was in pretty good condition.

When Type C hepatitis turns into cirrhosis, hyaluronic acid increases. However, with this patient it was a little higher than the average. The tumor marker for liver cancer, alphafetoprotein, was not too bad. The CT scan showed that the cancer was not spreading or getting bigger. Using an anticancer drug just because a patient has cancer helps him improve only temporarily and tends to make his condition worse later because of the drug reaction. I myself don't take this approach.

Mr. T's latest data show that alphafetoprotein was 13.6 (normal is less than 20) and hyaluronic acid was 102, which was twice as much but still relatively low for him, considering that he has cirrhosis. His Type C hepatitis antigen would not disappear. But if the biochemistry data such as hyaluronic acid, alphafetoprotein, and transaminase are normal, we can consider that he is completely cured.

Unfortunately, I was not strict enough with him about his eating habits. He was drinking, smoking, and eating foods he was not supposed to eat. His condition has worsened a little bit lately. The patient himself realizes what he has done to himself because of his bad habits. However, he is in good condition. In 1994 his GOT and GPT were both less than 50, and other tests showed normal results. He seems to be in good health recently.

MR. T— "AMAZED TO RECOVER FROM DISEASES I HAD, DUE TO MY INTEMPERANCE..."

I had Type B hepatitis and high blood pressure and continued to go to the Kosei Hospital near my house, taking medication given to me by the hospital for several years in order to lower my blood pressure.

I was diagnosed as having Type B hepatitis about 20 years ago, when I was age 37 or 38. I am not sure of the infection route, but I think I was infected in Manchuria when I was a child. At that time we had to be on watch at night without sleeping in fear of a U.S. air raid. The school provided methamphetamine and instructed us to inject it, so we injected about 2 cc every day.

By the time I returned to Japan, I was addicted to methamphetamine and injecting 250 cc per day. Despite advice from my seniors to give it up, I could not for a very long time. Finally, I managed to give it up. I was told by the hospital that my hepatitis was due to drug abuse, and I am sure that it was caused by the injections I was giving myself then.

In May 1992 1 fell unconscious because of acute diabetes and came to Dr. Tsurumi. My eyesight had gone quite bad before I fell unconscious, but I did not feel fatigue or any other distinct symptoms of diabetes. My eye blurred, so I bought a diabetes testing kit at a pharmacy and checked it by myself; the result was negative.

I said to myself that I didn't have diabetes after all and kept on working. I started getting abnormally thirsty and kept drinking water. The amount I was urinating per day was approximately five to six sake bottles (one bottle is 1.8 liters). I had a good appetite and ate a lot, but then I would go to the bathroom right after eating. I started wondering if my condition was abnormal. Then, I could not walk any more. I was told for a long time to meet Dr. Tsurumi, but my working schedule did not allow me to do so until now.

At Dr. Tsurumi's clinic, I was told for the first time that I had diabetes, and because of low blood sugar and dehydration, I lost consciousness. After consultation, I started drinking high energy Pi-Water that day, and about one week later I felt better and my body felt light. My blood pressure was still high, but it has gone down to a normal range although I did not take any drugs to lower it. Right now I do not have any problems as far as diabetes is concerned. As for the hepatitis, I started drifting back to my intemperate habit once I began to get better, and it got worse again. However, owing to Dr. Tsurumi, who introduced me to Pi-Water, I have no trouble leading a normal daily life.

Case Reports by Dr. Harutomo Tomori,
Toyo Clinic (Toyota City, Aichi Prefecture)

Ms. Y, AGE 57, A LIVER CANCER PATIENT

Ms. Y had surgery to remove a part of her lung in 1964 when she had tuberculosis. Blood transfusion was given during the operation. In February 1992 she developed jaundice and was diagnosed as having Type C (viral) hepatitis from the blood transfusion she received in surgery.

Ten months later she was diagnosed with cirrhosis at a hospital in Hokkaido. Then she developed liver cancer. According to the statistics, about one third of the patients having the virus-related hepatitis will develop liver cancer. Unfortunately, she was one of them.

Many doctors use interferon, which is called the latest treatment, to treat hepatitis. Interferon is an expensive medicine, costing about ¥60,000 per shot, and so doctors do not use it for seriously ill patients because it is unlikely to be effective even if a high dose of it were given to them. Present national (Japanese) medical expenses surpass ¥20 trillion. The Ministry of Welfare spelled out its policy to cut down national medical expense: seriously ill patients were not to be given expensive medication.

The doctors had given up on this patient because of the above constraints and she decided to come to my clinic in August 1992. Ms. Y's examination data before she was given high energy Pi-Water showed GOT of 126 (normal is 35) and GPT 3 (normal is 28). Some of the tumor markers were high. After she began taking Pi-Water, these figures started to decrease. By February her

TABLE 4.3 - MS. Y., 57, LIVER CANCER

Amount of high-energy Pi-Water given: 100 drops per day to 2000ml
purified Pi-Water as of August, 1992

		Before Pi-Water was Given	After Pi-Water was Given				
DATE OF EXAM		8/4	11/12	11/26	1/18	1/25	2/2
ITEM OF EXAM	NORMAL FIG.	EXAM FIG.			EXAM FIG.		
GOT	5-35IU/I	126↑↑	70	67	58	62	57
GPT	4-28IU/I	73↑	51	44	41	43	39
γ-GPT	4-42IU/I	43↑	40 N	34 N	32 N	38 N	42 N
T. P	6.1-8.1g/dl	8.1 N	7.7 N	6.8 N	6.9 N	7.3 N	7.1 N
ZTT	2-11.2KUU	13.3↑	10.6 N	10.1 N	10.6 N	11.1 N	11.2 N
T. C	135-230mg/dl	193 N	162 N	149 N	143 N	159 N	153 N
IAP	275-570mg	287 N					
CEA-S	Below 2.5mg	Below 1.0 N					
AFP	Below 20mg/dl	19 N	53.8↑↑			22.2	
CA19-9	Below 36U/mg	29 N					
Ferritin	10-80mg/ml	59 N					
DUPAN2	Below 150U/mg		154↑			164↑	169↑
TPA	Below 125U/g		321↑↑			104↓	103↓

*N means normal figure

GOT was 57, and her GPT was 39. They were almost normal.

Tumor markers are AFP, CA19-9, ferritin, DUPAN2, TPA. Health insurance only covers up to three, so considering her financial burden, I examined the ones I thought would be most critical. They were ferritin and CA19-9, and they turned out to be normal. In the second exam, AFP was high. In the third exam, DUPAN2 and TPA levels seemed abnormal. This meant that the cancer reaction had turned positive.

If I did all the exams at once, from the beginning, they would have shown higher figures. Although I could not do so under the circumstances, all the monthly figures were clearly moving closer to normal ranges. The results of almost all the items in February showed that they were normal. DUPAN2 was the only one that was left to return to normal. The fact that this is higher means she still has positive cancer reaction, but with continued treatment, all the levels are beginning to turn to normal. (See Table 4.3: Ms. Y., 57, Liver Cancer.)

MR. C, AGE 54, A RECTUM CANCER PATIENT

This patient had lower abdominal pain and bloody feces in October 1991 but did not receive any treatment. In March 1992 he had acute pain in his abdomen and was rushed to a public hospital in Hokkaido, where extensive surgery removed all of his rectum, including the anus, as well as a part of his liver since cancer had spread to it. The doctors constructed a man-made anus for him. The cancer had spread to his bladder as well, but the doctors decided to preserve it in order to lessen the trouble and pain the patient would have had to go through.

Mr. C was discharged from the hospital in May 1992, but during his regular checkup in August, a CT scan revealed that the cancer had spread in his liver, and he was hospitalized again. Since they could not remove any more liver, all they could do was inject an anticancer drug into his liver artery and close the opening that they had made in the surgery. They told him that he had until November or so to live.

In October 1992, with a letter from his family doctor at Rosai Hospital in Hokkaido, he came to my clinic. In the letter, his doctor explained in detail about the surgeries the patient had undergone, the names of the anticancer drugs he had taken, and the other various medicines that he had been taking. His doctor tried to treat this patient the best he could, whereas other doctors might have given up long before. I gave him a large amount of high-energy Pi-Water and an immune treatment at the same time. Since anticancer drugs lower immunity, it is such a troublesome medicine for someone like me, a doctor who treats patients so that their immunity improves. I never use any anticancer drugs.

After only four months of treatment, all of his cancer disappeared. Now he is even engaged in heavy manual labor, which makes me extremely happy. In fact, he owes a lot to his wife, who truly wished and helped aid his recovery Let me tell you about her. We will discuss more about her in the next case.

MS. Y, AGE 53, A SYSTEMIC LUPUS ERYTHEMATOSUS PATIENT

Mr. C's wife, Ms. Y, has been suffering since she was 29 years old

TABLE 4.4 – MS. Y.H., 58, SYSTEMIC LUPUS ERYTHEMATOSUS (SINCE 29 YEARS OLD)

Date of Exam / Item of Exam	Normal Fig.	Before Pi-Water was given		After Pi-Water was given	
		1991.7 Exam Fig.	1992.8 Subjective Symptom	1993.7 Exam Fig.	1993.8 Subjective Symptom
RBC	F345-460x10^4	320↓	Living only indoors	417 N	18 methods at shrine every morning
WBC	F31-88x10^4	9100↑	No housework	6300 N	All housework and shopping possible
Hb	F10.1-14.6g/dl	7.2↓	Walking was hard, crawl up stairs	11.8 N	Walk 5-15km/week
Ht	F31-43%	22.8↓	Right leg joint fixed	36.2 N	Go hiking sometimes
BSR 1h	2-15mm	120	Right hand joint movement limited	52↑	Slightly limited movement of knee
BSR 2h	2-30mm	150	Raynaud's phenomenon on toes	96↑	Can turn ankles and wrists
RF	Below 35U	700	Stiff shoulders	10 N	Raynaud's phenomenon (–)
UA	2.5-6.7mg/dl	6.9	Lower back pain	16.9 N	Slight headache
BUN	8-20mg/dl	29↑	Severe headache	1.09 N	Stiff shoulders
Cr.	0.4-1.1mg/dl	1.6↑	No appetite	7.9 N	Lower back pain
T.P	6.1-8.1g/dl	6.8 N	Bottom erosion	10 N	Normal appetite
GOT	5-35 IU/I	15 N	Negative thinking, depressed	0.1 N	No bottom erosion
GPT	4-28 IU/I	7 N	Not talkative		Better complexion
CRP	Below 0.6mg/dl	4↑			Positive thinking
Fe	48-170mg/dl	34↓			Bright and active

NOTE: N means normal

from systemic lupus erythematosus, a kind of collagen, or connective tissue, disease that is designated one of the most difficult diseases. She has pain all over her body because of multiple arthritis and Raynaud's phenomenon, which causes blood to stop flowing in peripheral arteries. The worst symptom she has is stiffness in the joints of her right leg combined with the symptoms of Raynaud's phenomenon. If she ignored the problem, then her leg will start to rot. She was told that she had to have her leg amputated in order to suppress any further development of the disease.

She came to me asking me to write a referral letter to the hospital, explaining that she needed to have her leg cut off at her joint. I talked to her for a while about various possibilities, and then I began treating her and encouraging her that her disease could certainly be cured.

She had so many symptoms at that time. She had collagen disease to begin with, along with stiff shoulders, lower back pain, lack of appetite, negative thinking, anemia, and rheumatism. She had an erosion on her buttocks since she had to move around on her bottom. Her left ankle was worn because she always put weight on there, but she did not have anything wrong with her liver.

I gave her high energy Pi-Water and an alternative treatment. A year later, she was completely cured. She was able to use a Japanese-style toilet and she could walk 15 kilometers and even run. Now I encourage her to do *kiko* and consciousness improvement and direct her to deal with her life with a positive attitude. (See Table 4.4: Ms. Y.H., 58, Systemic Lupus Erythematosus (Since 29 Years Old).)

MR. A , AGE 53, A DIABETES PATIENT

This patient was hospitalized on June 4; he came to my clinic through a friend's introduction at the beginning of July. He started taking high energy Pi-Water and alternative treatment. However, the hospital discharged him because these treatments are against the treatment policies of the hospital.

Generally, the hospital staff use insulin for serious diabetes patients to lower the blood sugar. This is not really a treatment, though. It is

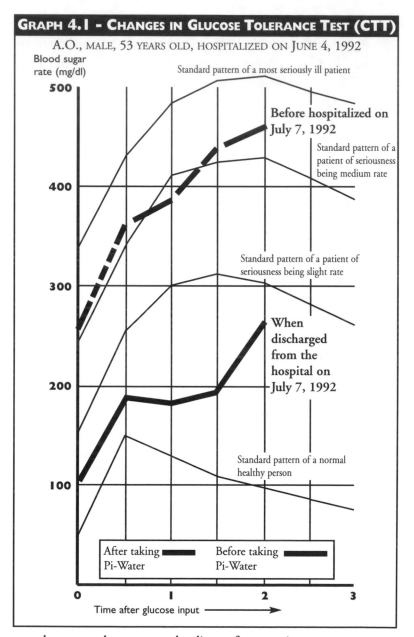

GRAPH 4.1 - CHANGES IN GLUCOSE TOLERANCE TEST (CTT)

A.O., MALE, 53 YEARS OLD, HOSPITALIZED ON JUNE 4, 1992

Blood sugar rate (mg/dl)

Standard pattern of a most seriously ill patient

Before hospitalized on July 7, 1992

Standard pattern of a patient of seriousness being medium rate

Standard pattern of a patient of seriousness being slight rate

When discharged from the hospital on July 7, 1992

Standard pattern of a normal healthy person

| After taking Pi-Water | Before taking Pi-Water |

Time after glucose input →

merely a control to prevent the disease from getting worse.

I used high energy Pi-Water and alternative treatment on this patient. When he was discharged from the hospital on July 7 and examined several days later, all the test data showed no problems.

There are many diabetes patients besides this man who are able to improve tremendously with this treatment. The important point in treatment is helping patients improve their quality of life. (See Graph 4.1: Changes in Glucose Tolerance Test (CTT).)

MR. L, AGE 80, A DIABETES PATIENT

This patient is 80 years old with a blood sugar level of over 400. I had him take high energy Pi-Water after he got into a hospital. For various personal reasons he stopped taking it for a while, at which point his blood sugar rate started to go up, eventually reaching the level he was at before he was hospitalized.

AMAZING EFFECT EXPERIENCED WITH PI-WATER
MR. K OF NISHIO-CITY, AICHI PREFECTURE—THREE YEARS OF DIALYSIS

It has been three years since I started dialysis, and I have been really suffering from this painful treatment plus strict diet limitations, such as controlled intake of salt and water. Sometimes I feel as if my body and my life are controlled by a machine. Sometimes my complexion is so bad that I get embarrassed about seeing other people. I cannot bear to look as myself in the mirror when my black face swells up.

One day, someone told me about Pi-Water, so I started drinking it, not really believing completely in its effects. I have a limit to what I can drink, so it took me a while to decide to drink it. But I ended up drinking two glasses of Pi-Water at a time, and I drank it twice a day.

Those of us who are suffering from diabetes cannot urinate much, and the doctors decide on the amount of liquid we can take in. When we go to see a doctor for the first time, he or she weighs us and decides upon an appropriate, or base, weight for us; then we must be careful that our weight does not exceed that base weight. If our weight is more than that base weight when we go in for dialysis, the technicians remove the same amount of water as the weight increase.

About two weeks after I started drinking Pi-Water, I noticed that I was able to urinate better. Encouraged by this change, I continued drinking it, and then after about two months or so, I was able to urinate about one liter a day. I was amazed and really glad. In my case, I have dialysis once every two days. I am really well before the treatment, but afterward, I feel exhausted and have no energy at all. I don't know what is wrong. In fact, I am just as well as a healthy person before the dialysis. A friend of mine referred me to a doctor who uses Pi-Water treatments. The doctor explained after listening to my background that "we decided upon a basic weight for you when you are in the worst condition, before you start dialysis. When you get a little better and you have more appetite, you will naturally begin to gain weight. Why don't you talk to your doctor about raising your baseline weight a little?" But I had a tough time talking to my doctor for a while. Finally I decided to ask him to raise my base weight. He raised it by only 200 gm and my condition greatly improved.

The friend who introduced Pi-Water to me says that I should decrease the frequency of dialysis, but the hospital won't allow me to do so. At any rate, my complexion and my overall conditions are the same as they were when I was healthy. I have a much improved appetite, and I am very thankful.

MR. D, AGE 39, OF MIDORI WARD, KANAGAWA PREFECTURE— DIABETES CURED WITHOUT HOSPITALIZATION

I am a freelance writer for weekly magazines. I used to have terrible habits such as drinking, smoking, and eating at irregular eating times.

One day after work, I got into a taxi and realized that my eyes were terribly blurred. I thought maybe it was because of my heavy drinking at a party previous night, and I didn't do anything about it. The next day, I could not even stay on my feet and felt really sick. I hurried to the hospital where the doctor said that my blood sugar was dangerously high at 250 and that I needed to be hospitalized at once.

I could not take any days off from work, but I managed to go home that day. When I told a friend of mine about my condition, he told me to drink Pi-Water right away, and so I went to get it from him. He said, "Drink a lot and you will be better." I went out to get some mineral water and started drinking Pi-Water with it.

Two or three days later, I felt better. A week later, I went back to the hospital to have my blood sugar tested, and it had gone down to 150. I really wondered how my blood sugar had gone down without my taking any medication. The doctor also wondered why. All I did was simply drink Pi-Water. Encouraged by this result, I began to put Pi-Water in everything I ate and drank. Then when I went back for a checkup again a month later, my blood sugar rate was down to 80!

Since I have a job with irregular work hours, being absent for a long time because of sickness is a problem, and I am just so thankful that I was able to continue working. Recently I have been trying to eat regularly and not to drink or smoke as much. I tend to slip back into bad habits when I am in a good condition, so I have to keep telling myself that without my good health, I won't be able to work.

SKIN AND HAIR REVIVE WITH PI-WATER

Everyone—men and women—wishes to look young and keep himself or herself beautiful and healthy; this may be the eternal theme for human beings. Human skin ages for various reasons, including exposure to active oxygen and ultraviolet rays, but the main reason is that the energy of outer skin cells decreases over the years. When we give Pi-Water's aura energy to outer skin cells that begin aging, the cells are activated and become young again. In addition, one of the functions of aura energy is to eliminate active oxygen.

Pi-Water has various functions such as expanding adaptability, enhancing one's ability to revive, and improving living body functions. These are benefits that cosmetic products need to offer. In fact, a cosmetic cream with a Pi-Water system base works well on burns and cuts; they heal quite well within a short period of time when Pi-Water is applied to them. There are many other examples: spraying Pi-Water on the hair makes white hair disappear, and applying Pi-Water system skin lotion before and after swimming in the sea helps prevent serious sunburn; it also lightens spots and freckles.

A hairdresser used a hair care product with a Pi-Water system base and was totally amazed at its effect and quality. A salesman put Pi-Water skin lotion on only his left hand for a month, and he could see the difference between his left hand, which became very smooth, and his right hand, which remained unchanged.

Special circulatory equipment of the Pi-Water system is available to wash your hair. Using this equipment, you wash your hair with warm Pi-cleansing liquid, just as you would wash it in the shower. In the beginning the cleansing liquid is transparent; then within about 15 minutes, it turns as white as milk. The hair is totally clean, because it is washed thoroughly with shampoo before using this equipment. There is 300 cc of cleansing liquid initially, but after washing your hair, there is only 150 cc left. It cannot have evaporated within 15 minutes, so that means the liquid was absorbed by your hair and scalp. If you used tap water instead of Pi-cleansing liquid, about 70 to 80 cc of water would be absorbed. (Your scalp absorbs water whenever you wash your hair.) Use of a shampoo that contains a surface active agent enables water to be absorbed through your scalp into your body.

Every year many new hairdressers start working in this business. However, about 20 percent of them leave their jobs within the first few years. They love their jobs, but they can not stand the trouble they have with their hands. If you have to shampoo the hair of 20 to 30 people every day, you are bound to have red, swollen hands, and what is worse, your fingerprints may disappear as a side effect of exposure to the surface active agent in the shampoo. A surface active agent has a very high degree of penetration to help it clean better. Thus, while you are washing your hair, it will be absorbed through your hand, too. Sometimes, when a person who suffers from irritated hands begins using Pi-Water cleaning circulatory equipment, the ailment disappears. (See Figure 4.1: Normal scalp and Figure 4.2: Scalp after washing Pi-Water Circulatory Machine.) The Pi-Water system is not only significant for cus-

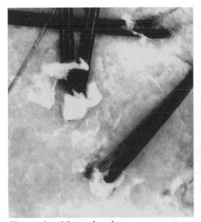

Figure 4.1: Normal scalp.

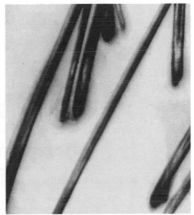

Figure 4.2: Scalp after washing Pi-Water Circulatory Machine.

tomers but also for hairdressers. These cosmetic products using the Pi-Water system are sold by Neway Japan Company, Ltd. and have a very good reputation. Above anything else, its contribution to hairdresser's improvement of health was the biggest achievement.

PI-WATER SYSTEM APPLIED TO WATER PURIFIER

About 70 percent of the human body is water, so drinking good quality water is a must for us all. However, when we talk about health today, we are first of all interested in medications. Very few people are aware of the importance of water. Now that the contamination of tap water has been shown to be a problem, such products as water purifiers and mineral water are drawing everyone's attention. It is good that people are becoming more interested in water, but it is important that they really understand the true importance of water.

The city of Osaka uses Lake Biwa as its source of tap water. Although people have been long concerned about the pollution of the lake, the rate of contamination has not really been reduced. In summertime, a large amount of algae grows in the lake, so even with the high speed filtration system at a filtration plant, it is impossible to remove the smell of the molds.

The number of diseases possibly caused by contamination of drinking water is on the increase. Unfortunately, however, very few people understand that the real cause of their diseases is water. In addition, it

TABLE 4.5 - WATER CLUSTER / ^{17}O-NMR HALF WIDTH	
Tap water (Hazu-cho, Aichi prefecture)	127.8Hz
Pi-Water purifier	53.2Hz
REFERENCE VALUES	
Original water	128.0Hz
(Water in which) ceramic ball is soaked	89.0Hz
(Water in which) magnetic iron ore is soaked	85.0Hz
(Water in which) BAKUHANSEKI is soaked	97.0Hz
(Water in which) extreme infrared radiation ceramic ball is soaked	89.0Hz
Alkaline electrolyte water	64.0Hz
SOURCE: FOOD AND DEVELOPMENT 24 (7), 82 ('89)	HZ: HERZ

may be difficult for a healthy person to believe that washing vegetables and fruits with tap water destroys vitamin C and other nutrients. It contributes to eczema and liver disorders and can trigger cancer.

Large amounts of chlorine are used to purify polluted water. Basically, chlorine is a byproduct of the process of producing caustic soda from salt. Chlorine costs very little, and it is the most suitable chemical to use for disinfecting tap water because it oxidizes, disinfects, and decolorizes. However, chlorine has a history of being used by the German military to produce poisonous gas, and with multiple contamination, it generates trihalomethane, which is a cancer-causing chemical.

In order to clean contaminated tap water and as an alternative to chlorine, simple water purifiers have become very popular and are selling really well. Active carbon and hollow fibers are used for such purifiers. Active carbon eliminates organic substances causing bad smells. Hollow fibers eliminate various bacteria.

Is it satisfactory just to eliminate bacteria and bad smell from tap water? In agriculture, the vicious cycle is that we are using more chemicals to supplement the lost energy of the soil. Soil energy was lost because we used too much agricultural chemicals to begin with. The same happens with water. Because so many chemicals are used in the filtration plant in order to disinfect water and eliminate the bad smell, that water loses its original energy. Therefore, this water cannot be good for us.

Various natural water sources around Japan, such as underground water and hot springs, are all effective purifiers because of the energy that they have. However, it is not the components making up the water that cure diseases.

The water purifier with Pi-ceramics, made with the Pi-Water system, has been developed to raise energy in water. When we take a Kirlian photograph in order to see how much energy the Pi-ceramic contains, a very strong aura is emitted. Since water goes through such strong energy, it can store energy that is quite strong, too.

After water receives strong aura energy from the Pi-ceramic, its clusters become extremely small. At present, we cannot measure the change in the sizes of clusters. Therefore, generally it is measured with a half width of nuclear magnetic resonance spectrum, ^{17}O-NMR. The smaller the figure is, the smaller the clusters are.

As shown in Table 4.5: Water Cluster/^{17}O-NMR Width, the tap water in Hazu-cho, Aichi prefecture, where I live, is 128 Hz. Clusters of water that went through the water purifier with Pi-ceramic were reduced tp 53.2 Hz. We can say that the size of the clusters in this water is one of the smallest in the world.

Pi-Water can cause a number of phenomena to occur. Just by drinking water from this purifier, some people eliminated problems such as eczema and hay fever. Pets that drank the water had shiny coats, and their feces stopped smelling bad. Orchids became healthy, free from diseases, and had more flowers. These are just a few examples.

Pi-Water can also retain freshness of vegetables; remove agricultural chemicals; and improve the taste of coffee, rice, and watered whisky. As for the whisky and water, some people had fewer problems with hangovers.

The Pi-Water purifier is not just a mere purifier. The Pi-Water purifier belongs to a completely new category because it gives energy to water.

CHAPTER FIVE

ENVIRONMENTAL POLLUTION

About 4.6 billion years ago, there was no ozone layer outside the atmosphere or stratosphere around the newly created earth. Therefore, harmful ultraviolet rays fell on the earth making the environment unable to sustain terrestrial life.

Life began eventually, however, in the ocean, which was not affected by the harmful ultraviolet rays. It was the first primitive plant *aimo,* a type of coral, that began producing oxygen by photosynthesis, using the earth's abundant carbon dioxide.

For several hundred million years since then, oxygen, which could be regarded as a kind of industrial waste, covered the earth. Oxygen reacted chemically with the ultraviolet rays from the sun and eventually formed the planet's ozone shield. There was now a filter around the earth that could cut off the sun's harmful ultraviolet rays, making it possible for the earth to maintain terrestrial life and leading eventually to the birth of human beings.

It took several billion years to reach this point. When we think of how old the earth is, the time when human beings came into existence was just a relatively short while ago. We human beings must make an effort to maintain the environment of the earth or improve it as much as possible. This is the mission that has been entrusted to humans. If we continue to lead our lives as we have been thus far, satisfying our needs and greed, the earth's environment will deteriorate, becoming a planet where no creatures can live. Signs of this are already visible. For example, *aimo,* the species of coral that began producing precious oxygen for the earth, only exists now in the sea near Perth in western Australia.

We regard the evolution of human beings as a development of science. Our advancement has brought us a convenient lifestyle. For instance, the only means of transportation used to be on foot. Now airplanes take us wherever we want to go in a very short time. Only 100 years ago, it used to take one or two months by ship to get to Australia from Japan. Now it only takes about nine hours. However, to enjoy this convenient lifestyle, we continue to destroy the earth's environment, and now the very survival of humankind is in danger.

Nitrogen oxide emitted from jet planes and automobiles and freon gas commonly found in air conditioners have contributed to the depletion of the ozone layer. At the same time, consumption of petroleum, a fossil fuel, continues to increase. These factors cause drastic changes in the ecosystem.

Basically, our very existence on earth leads to environmental pollution. We grow grains, vegetables, and fish and kill animals in order to satisfy our daily eating needs. If the food supply and demand are extremely unbalanced, that affects the ecosystem. Also, the laundry detergent that we use pollutes rivers and oceans. Recently chemicals used for agriculture have also become a serious problem.

POLLUTED WATER SURROUNDING US

The water sources for large cities, such as the Arakawa and Edogawa Rivers in Tokyo and Lake Biwa that supplies water to the city of Osaka, are totally contaminated. Their water quality is the worst in Japan. Because of poor quality water at the supply sources, we have to disinfect it with strong chemicals such as chlorine in order to make it into potable water.

Well water is no exception; we can no longer drink it as we used to. Not only wells in Tokyo but those in the countryside are contaminated. Nowadays we can detect such agricultural chemicals as atrazine and trichloroethylene in most well water.

Underground water used to be the best quality drinking water. It contained a great deal of energy because it passed through a natural filter system of soil and rocks. However, all the chemicals used in rice or vegetable fields and golf courses has now filtered into underground aquifers, thus contaminating water.

Human beings have been polluting the most important elements we need to support our lives—our environment and water. The relationship between living creatures and water has been extremely close ever since the earth was created. Thanks to water the environment has become naturally suitable for life.

As mentioned earlier, human history is extremely brief in comparison to the history of the earth. Human beings who lived

10,000 years ago did not have advanced medicine. However, they may have been healthier than we are today because they lived in an ecologically well balanced, living environment filled with energy.

What we need to think about here is that the most horrifying environmental pollution is contamination of the water. When we drink contaminated water, our bodies cannot avoid being affected since more than 60 percent of human body is water.

Nostradamus predicted that human beings will perish in July 1999. Will we perish because of diseases caused by the unbalanced ecosystem that is the result of water and air pollution? Recently a new kind of virus was discovered in England that causes parts of some humans' skin to die. These new strains of virus, including the AIDS virus, seem to be telling us that something is wrong.

We must create an environment where we can easily obtain clean, good quality water in order for all the people in the world to lead healthy lives. It is our mission to find out what we can do to achieve this goal. The Pi-Water that we will talk about in this book will certainly provide one of the solutions to this serious problem.

ENVIRONMENTAL POLLUTION AND NEW DISEASES

At the Kyoto University Primates Center, located in Inuyama city of Aichi Prefecture, they study the largest species of monkey. About ten years ago, there were a number of deformed monkeys without legs born one after another at this center. To the scientists' surprise, there were also many deformed monkeys born at exactly the same time at a number of different locations. The scientists learned the cause of this problem was the agricultural chemical used on apples, which were part of the monkeys' daily diet.

There were many deformed fish in Minamata Bay after chemical plants discharged mercury into the bay. A similar problem occurred in Ise Bay at the time of the Yokkaichi pollution. In these cases, investigators were able to specify the material causing the pollution, so that the problems were not repeated later on. Unfortunately, present scientific technology often cannot detect the materials causing multiple contamination.

It has been less than 10 years since people started paying attention to the problem of dying pine trees because of longicorns, (insects that eat pine trees). The problem spread throughout the country over a short period of time. Many pine trees disappeared from the mountains in Japan. There was such a drastic change that the vegetation of Japanese mountains and forests was affected.

Through a study conducted later on, authorities found that the cause of this problem was a virus carried by the longicorns. Did the virus appear suddenly and cause the pine trees to die? Probably not. That virus has existed since ancient times, but the natural ecological balance prevented it from multiplying. One theory reasons that pine resin kept away longicorns, but lately pine trees have no longer been producing resin. The main reason for this seems to be soil, water, and air pollution. However, it is often impossible to specify what the real cause is.

Moreover, there are many different kinds of new diseases such as AIDS, atopic dermatitis, and hay fever (pollen allergy). Did these diseases exist 20 years ago? Definitely not, or at least not to the degree that they do today. For example, hay fever is said to be caused by cedar pollen. Is that really true? Cedar trees are useful and grow fast, and so they have been used a lot in recent years. Hay fever usually affects people living in large cities. Very few people who live in the country surrounded by many cedar trees have the problem. Obviously, hay fever is caused both by air pollution and cedar pollen.

Atopic dermatitis was regarded only as a skin problem in babies about ten years ago. It was said that sufferers of atopic dermatitis would grow out of this condition by the time they entered school. Now many people suffer from it even when they reach 20 or 30 years of age. The direct or indirect cause of atopic dermatitis is the mother's body itself and is related to the contamination of drinking water or food. There are many pregnant women whose amniotic fluid is totally black. It is frightening to think that without being aware of it, we are creating in our bodies the causes for atopic dermatitis or more serious diseases by eating and drinking contaminated foods and water.

Whenever new agricultural chemicals are developed, many experiments have to be repeated to confirm their effectiveness before approval can be obtained from the proper authorities. For example, tests have to be run to determine the safety of these chemicals, the length of time they may remain toxic, their tendency to cause deformity, and their possible carcinogenic effects. Even though they are the subjects of many experiments, they could still cause problems such as those deformed animals, dying vegetation, and new diseases.

Today the number of new problems and diseases is rapidly increasing. The most probable causes of these diseases are soil, water, and air pollution.

CHAPTER SIX

✽ ✽ ✽

APPLICATION OF PI-WATER
TO OUR ENVIRONMENT

RESTORING RIVER WATER

The problem of polluted rivers and lakes continues. Local self-governing bodies are having a difficult time addressing the problem, although volunteers have tried to organize a movement to clean up the rivers. Water pollution is the most urgent problem that we need to solve. However, to solve this problem, it is necessary to combine various technologies, which will take a long time.

To return water to its natural state, we must apply Pi-Water information to such devices as material filters and absorption apparatus in order for it to work most efficiently. On the other hand, if we were to introduce Pi-Water into certain bacteria, their functions would be activated.

We have already confirmed Pi-Water's effectiveness in cleaning waste water from chicken processing factories and in the filtration systems of fresh fish tanks of restaurants. However, we have not had the same results from the experiments that we conducted with rivers and lakes. It won't be impossible to use Pi-Water to clean our rivers and lakes because we have seen that it can turn waste water from chicken processing factories into clean water where fish can live. Nevertheless, it all depends on the way we use the information of Pi-Water.

RETURNING TO NATURE

Every spring wild geese return to Yamagata prefecture. Farmers have noticed that the geese seem to prefer the paddy fields treated with Pi-Water soil conditioner because there are more worms and mud snails there. The farmers were happy and said, "It is just like it was 30 years ago!"

The quality of the soil had previously deteriorated because of the continuous use of chemical fertilizers and other agricultural chemicals. The soil has weakened so much that even worms, snails, fireflies, and other insects were not able to live there.

When we spread Pi-Water soil conditioner on such soil, the productivity of the soil improved. As well, the living creatures that had disappeared over the years came back and multiplied quickly. There was a place in Aichi prefecture where a large number of fireflies appeared and caused quite a commotion within the local community. These phenomena were not coincidental; they were quite common in the places that used Pi-ingredient.

The foul odor of domestic animal feces is a problem in rural areas. However, if we incorporate Pi-Water ingredients into the drinking water or on the floor cover of the animal's cages, the smell of feces disappears. It is believed that the smell disappears because the fermentation pattern changes. Generally, it takes about six months to a year of fermentation for animals feces to be used as fertilizer; otherwise it would damage the plants. By taking advantage of this technology, we should be able to recycle both agriculture and stock raising.

When you keep vegetable scraps in a container, they start to smell bad and a black solution accumulates in the bottom of the container. If you sprinkle the Pi-Water ingredient over them, they will turn into black compost, and there will not be any bad smell or foul solution.

Thus, Pi-Water makes it easier (for plants) to return to nature, which may contribute to preventing the destruction of the natural environment.

PI-WATER BECOMING KNOWN OVERSEAS

For the past several years, Pi-Water has become known internationally. Here are a few examples.

United States

Dr. K is the director of a Catholic hospital and manager of four clinics. A patient with breast cancer was given high energy Pi-Water, and her cancer disappeared within three months. Dr. K is planning to build a 260-acre health resort where he will use the Pi-Water system. It is his dream to enjoy leisurely activities in the lake region while engaging in agriculture and stock farming.

In a biochemistry class at Purdue University researchers added the appropriate amount of Pi-Water to a Hela cell (a type of cancer cell) culture bed. The Hela cells died, and normal cells continued to multiply. The investigators have performed extensive clinical experiments on diseases other than cancer and obtained good results from all of them.

In California, Mr. S is working hard toward beginning a business dealing mainly with water purifiers, health drinks, and cosmetic products.

Hungary

The Pi-Water system has been used in agricultural fields in Hungary, which was a Communist country until a few years ago. An agricultural specialist and a well known businessman, Dr. L. Fulop, continuously works hard toward spreading information about the Pi-Water technology and its applications. He has experimented with the Pi-Water technology in the field of agriculture, stock farming, and wine making. He has been trying to use Pi-Water in the field of health care products.

In 1992 during the Olympic games in Barcelona, Spain, Hungarian athletes won five gold medals. These five gold medalists were all drinking high energy Pi-Water regularly.

Based in Hungary, the Pi-Water system is spreading toward eastern Europe. The company that Dr. Fulop runs, Hemotrade, was nominated to receive the International Venus Award. This award is given only to companies in the European Community bloc. Hemotrade is the first company to receive it outside the EC bloc.

Korea

A business currently in progress features products that include water purifiers, health drinks, and cosmetic goods.

In 1993 we exhibited Pi-Water system at the World Expo, "Taejon Expo '93," and received a considerable amount of attention and comments. High ranking officials from the government visited the pavilion They took a look at the Pi-Water system and said that if all is true, then "we will consider national support." Currently, they are about to evaluate Pi-Water mainly in the agriculture field. Pi-Water has become quite well known in Korea.

In other countries, such as Taiwan, China, Malaysia, and Canada, other activities have begun.

Pi water has a very extensive technical potential that can be used for various fields and uses. The essence of Pi-Water is the change that it causes in the atomic level, which is the very origin of all substances. You can see the importance of Pi-Water from the fact that the change involves conveying memory and information.

Materialism derived from Western civilization has separated religion and science, and science has developed without our consciousness. As the result, we have a serious problem with the earth's environment. I believe that Pi-Water will play an important role in uniting religion and science, which must come together.

Pi-Water may provide answers to problems that conventional science cannot solve. Therefore, it is impossible to protect this technology simply with a piece of patent paper. Pi-Water has such depth.

Pi-Water technology has already been applied to agriculture and industries overseas and proven itself to produce beneficial effects. In Japan, it is used in agriculture, industry, and many corporations to address the earth's environmental problems. However, this alone cannot solve all the problems we have with regard to our health and the earth's environment.

In order to face the 21st century effectively and efficiently, many institutions must study ways to apply the Pi-Water technology in order to prevent the deterioration of the earth's environment. It is essential that a national project be created for this purpose. One private institution cannot achieve such a huge goal alone.

CHAPTER SEVEN

❋ ❋ ❋

APPLICATION OF
PI-WATER TO
INDUSTRIAL INDUSTRIES.

You have seen that Pi-Water has amazing effects on plants and animals, but it can also benefit industry. One can comprehend the broad applications of Pi-Water better if one considers Pi-Water not just as regular water, but as an energy medium. The following are some examples of how it is applied in the industrial fields.

PI-WATER EFFECTIVE FOR FACTORY WASTE WATER TREATMENT

Waste water treatment is one of the most difficult problems within the chicken processing industry. Factory workers cut off the heads of thousands of chickens and discard them along with blood, fat, and other waste matter. As this material mixes with waste water, it turns the water red. When it is discharged, it becomes a major cause of river pollution. If we treat the waste water with the Pi-Water system, it turns into clean water that fish can live in without any problems.

We tested factory waste water as it was released into pipes to be filtered. The amount of filtration material was the same in two separate pipes. The only difference between the pipes was that one had Pi-information and the other did not. We clearly could see the difference between the filtered water that came from the pipe with Pi-information and the water that flowed out of the pipe without it. The efficiency of the filtration material with Pi-information was perfect. However, dirty water came out of the other system. These results occurred because the absorbent capacity of the filtration material increased with Pi-information, and it was able to turn the waste water into clean water.

METAL PIPES DO NOT RUST

To test the capability of Pi-Water technology to preserve metal pipes, we prepared and sealed two plastic bags, each containing a piece of cotton soaked with highly concentrated hydrochloric acid and a piece of iron pipe. One of the iron pipes had previously been treated with Pi-Water. Hydrochloric acid gas immediately filled up the plastic bags.

Twenty-four hours later, the untreated pipe was red with rust. However, there was no change in the treated pipe. It was still the same several months later.

THE STRENGTH OF CONCRETE IS INCREASED

Concrete for construction is generally made of natural sand from a river bed. However, lately there has been less and less river sand, for from the environmental protection point of view, it is difficult to obtain. Sand from the ocean could be used, but salt has to be extracted from it. It is easy to take salt out of a small amount of sand, but from a cost performance point of view, it is difficult to do so with a huge volume of sand.

Therefore, some concrete companies started to use andesite, a fine-grained rock, by breaking it to pieces. However, andesite rocks are alkaline, which causes cracks in the concrete. Thus, many of the shore protection concrete pieces and bridges kept cracking, which became a worldwide problem. However, when Pi-Water is used to mix concrete, not only there are no cracks but also the strength of the concrete is increased. More than a year later, there are no changes.

Additionally, because of acid rain, icicle-like projections develop on the concrete of highways and buildings, creating problems. If we are somehow able to come up with buildings that endure, we would be able to conserve resources and stop environmental pollution. (See Table 7.1: Mortar with Pi-Water Strength Test.)

TABLE 7.1 - MORTAR WITH PI-WATER STRENGTH TEST				
	7 DAYS LATER		28 DAYS LATER	
	BENDING	COMPRESSION	BENDING	COMPRESSION
Control Section	31kg/cm	137kg/cm	38kg/cm	178kg/cm
Treated Section	42kg/cm	170kg/cm	50kg/cm	225kg/cm

OCEAN WATER WITH PI-WATER DOES NOT FREEZE

Ocean water generally freezes when the temperature drops to about −20°C. Using the example of icebergs at the South and North Poles, we can see that ocean water can freeze and form huge masses of ice. However, ocean water containing Pi-Water does not freeze to form a solid mass of ice. It forms something like slush at −20°C. This is the result of changes that occur in water structure, that is, changes in the combination state.

DIESEL WASTE DECREASES CONSIDERABLY

The main cause of air pollution is fuel exhaust emissions from chemical plants and automobiles, particularly diesel exhaust. It was found through research conducted by the Tokyo Hygiene Institute that DEP (diesel exhaust particle) is a cause of lung cancer.

The Institute used 480 mice and inserted 0.05 g of DEP per week, collected from diesel exhaust, into their windpipes. After ten weeks, the researchers confirmed that 3 percent of the mice had malignant tumors in their lungs. The National Environmental Institute in Tsukuba city, Ibaraki prefecture, began their own experiments, suspecting that the diesel exhaust particle may cause asthma.

The chemical compound contained in DEP changes into active oxygen in the human body, which damages a specific gene. Lymphocytes generate active oxygen as well and try to get rid of the DEP, which speeds up the increase of cancer cells.

Exhaust gas also affects the ozone layer. The ozone layer is in the earth's stratosphere. It absorbs harmful ultraviolet rays from the sun, protecting the living creatures on the earth. However, all sorts of chemicals, such as exhaust gas (especially NOx) and freon used in spray products and air conditioning as a fire extinguishing agent, damage the ozone layer. If sunlight reaches the earth directly without being filtered through the ozone layer, it will cause health problems and destroy the ecological balance of the earth, affecting everything from plants to plankton.

To produce gasoline that causes less pollution, we tested the gasoline by adding the Pi-Water ingredient. The confirmed result was more than 20 percent improvement in mileage and considerably less carbon such as SO_2 and NO_2.

However, when we did that same test in Canada, mileage decreased by 15 percent. We cannot apply this to a practical situation, but researchers found it quite interesting to see the mileage going down as much as 15 percent just as a result of adding the Pi-Water ingredient. They think that there must be something causing such a reduction, and they are continuing their research. It is certain, though, that Pi-Water is very effective in filtering the exhaust gas that is emitted at the time the gasoline is being burned. Of course, we expect to see an improvement in mileage.

It is said that there are more than six million automobiles with diesel engines in Japan. Almost all of them emit harmful diesel exhaust gas. Mr. Sakamoto of Yagyu Industry, Kobe City, began his research sincerely hoping to decrease exhaust gas from diesel engines. He completed a revolutionary system, using the Pi-Water system. It is called the Energy Control System (ECS), and it considerably reduces DEP emissions from diesel engines. In addition, this system improves mileage by more than 60 percent. The black smoke test showed an average 45 percent decrease. We conducted a mileage test between Kobe and Tokyo. Before installing the system, the average mileage was 3.68 km/liter. After installing the system, it increased to 4.24 km/liter, a 15.2 percent increase.

We conducted a bench test at an industrial junior college. Before installing the system, the average mileage was 3.62 km/liter when driving 3 km, with the average speed of 60 km and average load of 35 kg., consuming 919 ml of gasoline. After installing the Pi-system, when driving 3 km at the average speed of 60 km, average load 40 kg, it took 443 ml of gasoline, or less than half of what it did before installing the system; the average mileage was 6.77 km/liter. This result alone shows very clearly that these systems using Pi-Water are not as harmful to the environment. (See Table 7.2: Combustion Efficiency Test by Installing Pi-system (Bench Test).)

TOXIC WASTE GAS FROM THE GARBAGE INCINERATOR DECREASES

Another cause of air pollution is the exhaust from garbage incinerators. It is dangerous because it contains various kinds of harmful materials. It is possible, however, to turn the emissions into a harmless exhaust gas by combining the Pi-Water system in the process of incineration. For example, the exhaust can be filtered through a Pi-Water shower.

TABLE 7.2 – COMBUSTION EFFICIENCY TEST BY INSTALLING PI-SYSTEM (BENCH TEST)			
	BEFORE INSTALLATION	AFTER INSTALLATION	IMPROVED RATE
Average speed	60.6km/h	60.6km/h	
Average load	20.2kg	20.0kg	
Fuel consumption	593ml	364ml	
Distance	3000m	3002m	
Average mileage	5.06km/l	8.24km/l	62.8% up
Average speed	60.3km/h	60.4km/h	
Average load	29.9kg	30.1km/h	
Fuel consumption	637ml	391ml	
Distance	3001m	3003m	
Average mileage	4.71km/l	7.68km/l	63.1% up
Average speed	59.4km/h	60.7km/h	
Average load	35.3kg	40.1kg	
Fuel consumption	919ml	443ml	
Distance	3001m	3001m	
Average mileage	3.26km/l	6.77km/l	107.7% up
Average speed		60.2km/h	
Average load		50.1kg	
Fuel consumption	invalid	529ml	
Distance		3000m	
Average mileage		5.67km/l	

These methods are not technically difficult once experts in the field are involved in the development. It is just a matter of time.

Pi-Water technology is drawing worldwide attention. Japanese companies are beginning to be interested and have developed and used various Pi-Water products. However, this is still just an initial stage for applying the Pi-Water system for practical use. At any rate, the basis of our healthy life is the purification of our natural environment. We must correct the very basic problems causing pollution of the soil, water, and air. Just paying attention to our health leads only to a temporary solution.

CHAPTER EIGHT

❋ ❋ ❋

APPLYING PI-WATER
TO AGRICULTURE

AGRICULTURAL REVOLUTION WITH PI-WATER

Our eating habits are becoming more healthful these days. Many people prefer foods without additives as well as organically grown vegetables, grains, and beans. For many food producers, "organically grown" and "contains no additives" are phrases that promote sales. However, are we really eating healthful foods?

For example, post-harvest chemicals used for imported rice in Japan present a serious problem. However, the only feature advertised seems to be how the Japanese people can enjoy eating imported rice. What really is good for our health is sadly forgotten here. There must be many reasons behind having to import rice. If we could improve Japanese agriculture, then we would not have to eat foods with so many chemicals. We don't pay much attention, however, to the fact that we are eating such foods because we don't seem to be affected by them right away. What if there are side effects in 10 years? We certainly don't want children and pregnant women eating such foods.

We must produce good food without agricultural chemicals. If we use Pi-Water in agriculture, we can expect it to be very effective. Let us look at several examples illustrating what happens when Pi-Water technology is applied to agriculture.

THE AMAZING EFFECT OF PI-WATER

Since Pi-Water was discovered by studying plants, it is naturally very effective for use on plants and vegetables. For example, if we soak seeds in Pi-Water seed treatment liquid, they grow very well after germination. Reproductive areas, such as roots, flowers, and seeds in particular, show tremendous effects. Also, the plant's adaptability to different environments improves considerably. These points are all proven by experiments from which we are able to obtain satisfactory results in reproductive tests. We can regard these phenomena as plant cells being activated by the aura energy supplied by Pi-Water, so that they grow as they are supposed to.

Today, worms cannot normally live in the water of a paddy field. However, in a paddy field where soil conditioner using Pi-

Water is applied, you find many worms. We are trying to determine whether the worm's adaptability improves with Pi-Water or if they are given an alternative energy source for breathing by Pi-Water.

TESTING VEGETABLES FOR THEIR TASTE AT HARVEST

Pi-Water has already been applied to agriculture in what is called a "Safety Agri-zone" in Hokkaido. Organically grown vegetables, such as potatoes, pumpkins, corn, and onions, are sold to families through several dealers. People enjoy the quality and taste of the new vegetables tremendously.

In addition to superior taste, vegetables grown with Pi-Water appear fresher and are easier to prepare and cook. These vegetables are also more nutritious in many cases. Thus, agricultural products with the Pi-Water application are perfect in all aspects.

PUMPKINS

Features: Glossy outer appearance, and the sarcocarp inside is quite thick and bright orange. They contain more than five times more carotene than pumpkins grown regularly. They can be stored for a long time.

Taste: Very sweet. The rate for sweetness is 13.7, which is about twice as high as regularly grown pumpkin (about 7.0). When wrapped in foil and baked in the oven, they taste sweeter than baked sweet potatoes. When you boil them, the outer skin becomes soft, but they will not break into pieces.

POTATOES

Features: The skin is whiter. There are fewer nodes.

Starch: 19.4 percent/100g (Usual rate: 16 percent/100g)

Vitamin C: 38 mg/l00g (Usual rate: 28 mg/100g)

They are more nutritious than regularly grown potatoes, and they are obviously of much better quality.

Taste: Very soft in the mouth. They have the special scent and taste of potatoes. There is less acid, so when used for salad, they would still taste just as good.

ONIONS

Features: They appear glossy from outside, and the size is even. The skin is easy to peel. They can be stored for a long time. It is confirmed with the electronic microscope that they are quite healthy and packed with many small cells.

Taste: They are easy to cut vertically or horizontally, and they taste good uncooked. The sweetness rate is 13 degrees, which is twice as high as regularly grown onions. They are sweet, crisp, and taste very good when put into salad. They do not fall apart easily when being boiled.

PI-WATER WIDELY USED IN AGRICULTURE IN CHINA

Pi-Water has already been applied in various aspects of agriculture in China. Several farmers in Dailen-city were quite surprised to see the results. In China *mou* is used as the unit for land measure. One *mou* is 660 square meters.

Growing cucumbers

Location: Lushunkou, Dailen-city, three greenhouses
Amount of Pi-substance sprayed: 60 kg/*mou*
Tested area: 0.9 *mou*
Comparison area: 1.2 *mou*

As Table 8.1 indicates, the treated area has very little downy mildew. Downy mildew is a plant disease that turns the leaves brown because of low soil fertility, which is caused by continuous use of the soil every year. The crop yield increased as much as 39 percent, just like the difference in the rate of the mildew.

					TABLE 8.1
DATE OF TESTING	NUMBER OF STUMPS	DOWNY MILDEW IN TREATED AREA	RATE OF DOWNY MILDEW	DOWNY MILDEW IN COMPARISON AREA	RATE OF DOWNY MILDEW
June 4	204	15	7.35%	32	15.68%
June 4	204	15	14.42%	19	18.26%
Total	308	30	9.74%	51	16.5%

Growing cucumbers
Location: Ganjinziqu, Dailen-city
One greenhouse is divided into three sections: treated area, control area, and area treated with anti-downy mildew medicine. The other greenhouse was sprayed with Pi soil conditioner. Results showed the cucumbers in the greenhouse where the whole greenhouse was treated with Pi soil conditioner grew better. There was less disease compared with those grown in the treated section of the other greenhouse. Compared with the section treated with anti-downy mildew agent and the control section, the section treated with Pi soil conditioner produced better growth and an extremely low rate of disease.

Growing tomatoes (See Table 8.2: Observation of Growth.)
Location: Ganjinziqu, Dailen-city
The soil quality was poor because of sea water and the salty breeze and showed pH 7-8. This is because the water contained a substantial amount of chlorine compound. Pi soil conditioner was applied to the soil, and later we observed improvement.

We observed the way tomatoes grew in the alkaline soil section treated with Pi-water soil conditioner. They grew much better than those grown in the control section (without treatment).

TABLE 8.2 - OBSERVATION OF GROWTH			
	CONTROL SECTION	TREATED SECTION	COMPARISON
Date Flowered	May 13	May 8	5 days earlier
Height of the stem	74.9 cm	81.2 cm	Average 6.3 cm higher
Thickness of the stem	5.5 cm	6.96 cm	Average 1.39 cm thicker

Growing eggplants (See Table 8.3: The Rate at Which Downy Mildew Occurs.)
Location: Xinnin, Liaoning
Amount of Pi-Water soil conditioner sprayed: Pi soil conditioner was equivalent to 1 percent of soil for growing seedlings.

In the treated section the occurrence of downy mildew was

TABLE 8.3 - THE RATE AT WHICH DOWNY MILDEW OCCURS		
	TREATED SECTION	CONTROL SECTION
Number Researched	42	42
Number affected by mildew	7	14
Rate affected by mildew	16.6%	33%
Disease affecting immunity	NO	YES

one half that of the control section. There was no disease affecting the plant's immunity. This result clearly shows the Pi-Water soil conditioner could help prevent mildews and diseases and improve immunity of the plants and soil.

GROWING TASTY RICE WITHOUT CHEMICALS

Rice is a food staple in Japan. Therefore, agricultural methods to improve production and ensure quality are essential.

There are quite a few farmers, all over Japan who use Pi-Water-based soil conditioner. They were able to improve the average production in some cases despite irregular weather—a particularly cool summer or warm winter, for example.

Ryoichi Kaneko of Fukushima prefecture used Pi-Water soil conditioner to produce 17 bags of rice per *tan* (9.92 acres). Average yield of rice per *tan* is about six to seven bags. Therefore he produced more than twice the average. Farmers talk about the "dream of 16 bags," which is regarded as impossible, and nobody has yet beaten Mr. Kaneko's record. However, when he achieved this, nobody believed him. It is unfortunate that producing six to seven bags per *tan* is regarded as average and taken for granted by the government. Mr. Kaneko overturned the conventional teaching of his local cooperative group. He theorized a method of producing more rice and devised a system that enables anyone to improve rice production yields. He succeeded in growing much more rice with thick, round stems and many roots.

In order to address the temperature changes caused by irregular weather, he came up with the method of controlling climate with water. He figured out how many leaves should be under water and when to add fertilizer. His method is so easy that the

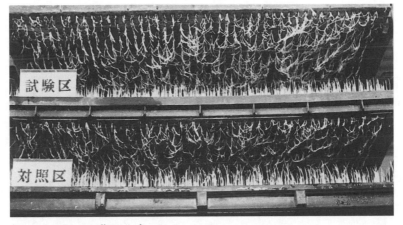

Figure 8.1: Rice seedlings in boxes.

beginner can produce rice without chemicals. However, many farmers were opposed to using this method because they thought it would ruin the rice. However, it was successful. If you grow rice, using Pi-Water soil conditioner increases the yield, improves the taste, and makes production easier. People who are not eating much rice may return to eating it again. Many think people prefer to eat less rice not just because the Japanese diet has become Westernized but because the rice itself has become less tasty.

Let us examine what kind of phenomena occur while growing rice using Pi-Water soil conditioner. We plant rice after growing seedlings to a certain size. The most important part is how we grow rice from the seeds. If this initial step is not good, then it would affect the eventual yield. We conducted an experiment to see how the seedlings grew. The testing section treated the seeds with Pi-Water, and in the control section, we grew rice in the conventional way.

Several weeks later, under the seedling box in the testing section we saw strong white roots. (See Figure 8.1: Rice seedlings in boxes.) There were not very many from the control section. However, the number of the leaves in the control section was a greater number than that of the testing section. On the surface, the control section seemed to be doing better. However, the activation of the plants does not show in the leaves but in the roots.

Therefore, if there are many strong roots, they would be able to absorb nutriments better; it is a mistake to judge the growth rate just by looking at the growth of the leaves. Then we transplanted the rice. For plants, the initial stage is very important—just as it is for human beings.

When transplanting the seedlings to the paddy field, we designated the area treated with Pi-Water soil conditioner as the testing section and the paddy field without treatment as the control section. Then, we applied twice as much nitrogen fertilizer to the testing section than we gave to the control section. The control section was given conventional fertilizer. The rice in the testing section, with twice as much nitrogen fertilizer, grew faster and much better. Many farmers would never use twice as much nitrogen fertilizer because they would fear the rice would die.

Plants are the same as humans. A healthy child would grow normally, having a good appetite and eating a lot of food. An unhealthy child has a poorer appetite and would only eat a little. When using Pi-Water, it is important to carry out appropriate control of fertilizer and water. When these factors are all carried out according to direction, tremendous results can be achieved. This is true not just in the field of agriculture but in other fields as well.

TESTING PADDY FIELDS IN SHIKOKU, JAPAN

Soil conditioner was used in the soil of the testing section. We applied conventional fertilizer to the control section; the testing section was given twice as much nitrogen fertilizer as the control section. We borrowed a part of the paddy field for this test. Farmers said that in such a windy area, the stems of rice would fall, and with twice as much nitrogen fertilizer, the rice would be affected by rice blast, a disease in which black spots appear on the rice and kill the plants. So the farmers advised us not to do the test. We listened to their advice but waited for the rice to grow.

All the rice in the control section fell. This was the area where conventional fertilizer control was used. (See Figure 8.2: Pilot farm in Shikoku Island, Japan.) However, the rice in the testing section where we applied twice as much nitrogen fertilizer was

Figure 8.2: Pilot farm in Shikoku Island, Japan.

still standing. The rice in the testing section had many strong roots as well as thick, round stems and obviously looked very healthy. There was also a big difference in the yield of the crops.

When using Pi-Water, it is important to maintain appropriate control of fertilizer and water. When these factors are all carried out in a positive manner, farmers can achieve tremendous results. This is true not only in the agriculture industry but also in any other fields as well.

DIFFERENCE IN THE RICE HARVEST YIELD

We conducted research on the yield of rice in only Gifu prefecture. We set up the testing section with seedlings that had been treated with Pi-Water before planting and the control section with regular seedlings. We did not use soil conditioner in either section. The amount of harvest in the control section was 10.31 bags per *tan* average, and that of the testing section was 13.21 bags, making about a 30 percent difference. The seeds used in the testing section were soaked in Pi-Water only for 10 minutes.

THE AMOUNT OF HARVEST IS IN PROPORTION
TO THE NUTRITION GIVEN

We tried to find out the relation between nitrogen fertilizer applied and the amount of harvest. We used a conventional way

TABLE 8.4 - EFFECT OF NITROGEN FERTILIZER WITH PADDY

	TREATED SECTION	TESTING (1) SECTION	TESTING(2) SECTION
Size of the Section	3.5a	11a	12a
NITROGEN CONTAINED PER 10A			
Original Amount of fertilizer	4.0	4.6	4.2
Additional Amount of fertilizer			
No. 1	1.4	2.2	2.0
No. 2	-	1.1	1.5
No. 3	-	2.7	-
Total	5.4	10.6	7.7
Date of Transplanting	April 21	April 20	April 21
Date when ears came out	July 5	July 5	July 5
Date of harvest	August 12	August 12	August 12
Number of bags per TAN	8.7	14.0	10.8
Harvest index	100	161	124

of fertilizing in the control section. The conventional way means applying the usual, customary amount of fertilizer for the particular soil since the makeup and the amount of fertilizer depends totally on the soil of the area. In the testing section (1), we used twice as much nitrogen fertilizer as the amount applied to the control section.

The amount of harvest was compared with the index figure of 100 for the testing section. The amount of harvest in the testing section (1) was 161, 60 percent more than the testing section. We did not use as much nitrogen fertilizer in the testing section (2), so it was 124. You can tell that the amount of harvest increases in proportion to the nitrogen fertilizer given. We also found that soil conditioner or seed treatment alone would not effectively produce a better harvest. Nutrition for the plants, as expected, is necessary for improving the amount of crop harvested. (See Table 8.4: Effect of Nitrogen Fertilizer with Paddy.)

SOIL REGAINS FERTILITY

The most important element for a plant's growth is the soil. If the soil is weak, the amount of harvest naturally decreases. Unfortunately, we often spray more chemicals in order to improve production, and the foods produced in this vicious cycle are sold in supermarkets. Let us examine how the soil itself in a pineapple field changes each sowing.

The soil we used for testing was not in poor condition. It was reddish with iron oxide, but it would have been impossible, no matter how hard we tried, to grow good pineapples. When this red soil was treated with Pi-Water soil conditioner, however, the soil became black within several months because corrosion occurred in the soil. It is rare, however, to be able actually to see the change. It occurred simply because Pi-Water's energy activated the soil.

We analyzed the granular form of the soil. The smallest particle of the soil is clay, and the next smallest is silt (ooze). Next are sand and soil, which are larger, and then gravel. Good soil has a high content of clay and silt. The soil in the control section contained 1.28 g of clay per 100 g. In the testing section, the soil contained 4.80 g of clay per 100 g, or four times as much. A similar increase was seen in silt as well. Usually, soil specialists say that they do not believe these findings, because this kind of change would normally require 100 or 1,000 years to take place in the natural world. (See Table 8.5: The Change in the Amount of Silt and Clay Contained in the Soil with Soil Conditioner.)

Farmers spread a lot of phosphoric acid in their paddies and fields. The worse the soil is (volcanic ash, for instance) the more phosphoric acid the soil will absorb (more than 90 percent).

TABLE 8.5 - THE CHANGE IN THE AMOUNT OF SILT AND CLAY CONTAINED IN THE SOIL WITH SOIL CONDITIONER		
	SILT	CLAY
Control Section	9.53g/dry soil 100g	1.28g/dry soil 100g
Testing Section	14.00g/dry soil 100g	4.80g/dry soil 100g

TABLE 8.6 – THE CHANGE IN PHOSPHORIC ACID ABSORPTION INDEX OF THE SOIL WITH SOIL CONDITIONER

	PHOSPHORIC ABSORPTION INDEX
Control Section	1259
Testing Section	935

Therefore, plants can absorb only the remaining several percent. Without any kind of treatment, volcanic ash soil has a phosphoric acid absorption index of 1259. We added the Pi-Water soil improvement ingredient to this soil and measured it again several months later. The index decreased to 935. The decrease in the index itself was quite significant, considering how bad it was initially. When we showed this data again to a soil specialist, he did not believe us.

In the study of soil fertilization, scientists have been trying for a long time to develop a method to decrease the soil's phosphoric acid absorption rate. Specialists in this field have a fixed idea that the rate cannot change within a short time, and so it will probably take a long time for them to understand this. Despite what these specialists say, we have experimented and confirmed the data that show the phosphoric acid absorption rates have decreased in the soil of many different areas from Hokkaido to Kyushu as a result of the use of Pi-Water soil conditioner. (See Table 8.6: The Change in Phosphoric Acid Absorption Index of the Soil with Soil Conditioner.)

PI-WATER HELPS THE SOIL RETURN TO EARLIER CONDITIONS
We all know that the air, soil, and water on earth have been polluted; the situation is becoming quite dangerous. The agricultural soil has lost its initial energy because we have been abusing it with chemical fertilizer and agricultural chemicals. The consequence of this loss of energy is that the soil has been damaged and has lost its aggregated structure. This presents an extremely serious problem.

The aggregated structure of the soil means that the clay and organic matter combine to form bigger particles, which presents the best conditions for growing plants. Plants are free from diseases growing in these particles and are not affected by drought or sudden changes in climate because the particles retain water more effectively. Long ago, when agricultural chemicals or chemical fertilizer were not used at all, soil had a lot of energy and firm structure. In addition, crops had more resistance to drought and tasted better.

Major fertilizer manufactures know very well that the more chemical fertilizer we give to the soil the weaker it will become. However, in reality, they cannot come up with an alternative solution. Those who are seriously thinking about agriculture are trying to return the soil to its original state by using organic fertilizers. Since the soil aggregation is so weak and it takes such a long time for improvements to occur, scientists cannot achieve their goals easily. When the aggregated structure of soil is not in order, it will not drain water well, and plants grown in that soil will become more susceptible to diseases.

Soil aggregation takes a long time to occur. Generally it is said to take as long as 1,000 years. Therefore, if there is a change in the structural combination, it could lead to a life-or-death situation. However, if Pi-Water soil conditioner is applied to the soil that lost its aggregation, the soil returns to normal within several months.

In Brazil primeval forests are rapidly being turned into fields. When it rains, the surface soil erodes, leaving deep holes, some as deep as five to six feet. However, we have actually seen that such weak soil improves within a short period of time with Pi-Water base soil conditioner.

The environment always affects the growth of plants. In a healthy environment, a plant would have ten roots but perhaps only five in a poor environment. We try to solve the problems created by the bad soil by using chemicals. Then we must increase the amount of chemicals because of the side effects of the chemicals.

SURPRISING EFFECTS PROVEN BY ACTUAL DATA

Why does the aggregation that normally takes 1,000 years to develop take place within only several weeks when Pi-Water is used? The specialists are all surprised.

You may not be easily convinced that Pi-Water helps the plants to grow well and improves the crops as well as the taste. Therefore, we tried experimental procedures with Pi-Water that would be considered impossible in actual agriculture.

For example, there are many farmers already applying Pi-Water to their farms. However, there are minute differences in how to use it depending on what the farmers want to produce. There is room for improvement—with the application of Pi-Water to agriculture—in order to achieve a more powerful effect. However, Pi-Water offers a strong base for future potential. Here are just a few examples.

KOMATSUNA (SPINACH) WITHOUT FERTILIZER INJURY

We planted *komatsuna*, or spinach, in six different pots. We put Pi-Water soil conditioner in three of them as testing sections and regular soil in the other three, which we designated control sections. We put four times the regular amount of nitrogen fertilizer in all the pots. Normally, with this much chemical fertilizer, so-called fertilizer injury would occur, in which plants would wither and fail to grow. But the spinach in the pots with Pi-Water soil conditioner showed quite healthy growth. (See Figure 8.3: *Komatsuna* (spinach) shows difference in growth with Pi-Water soil conditioner.)

In another example a farmer in Saitama prefecture spread Pi-Water soil conditioner on his one-hectare field. He ran out of it

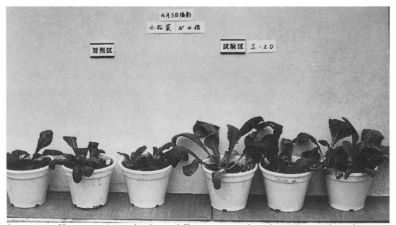

Figure 8.3: *Komatsuna* (spinach) shows difference in growth with Pi-Water soil conditioner.

Figure 8.4: Spinach free from problems caused by consecutive growth.

before being able to cover the whole field, thus, by chance, creating a testing section and a control section.

That year, there was a bad drought, and almost all the other farmers in that region lost their crops. The spinach in his control section also died. However, in the "testing" section, the spinach survived and was not affected at all by the drought. This was because the plants' roots grew deep into the ground and were able to secure water. If roots are short, they are naturally directly affected by drought.

GROWING SPINACH CONTINUOUSLY FOR 25 TIMES
Some crops stop growing well if we try to grow them continuously in the same field. Spinach is one of them. With a farmer in Tokorozawa city, Saitama prefecture, we did an experiment to see if Pi-Water could help overcome this problem.

Generally, spinach does not grow well when it is planted for the fourth consecutive time in the same field. Moreover, its production drops considerably. In the testing section of the greenhouse, the experiment was a success because we used Pi-Water soil conditioner. At the tenth consecutive planting, the spinach still grew quite well. The experts were very surprised to see this. We have confirmed planting's healthy growth up to the twenty-fifth consecutive time on the same field. (See Figure 8.4: Spinach free from problems caused by consecutive growth.)

Figure 8.5: Pineapple leaves were so thick in the testing section that we could not see the ground.

With Pi-Water soil conditioner, spinach can be grown free from the troubles associated with consecutive growth. In the same experiment, we added nitrogen fertilizer, which was ammonium sulfate. Too much ammonium sulfate acidifies the soil. This field had pH that showed strong acidity. However, the amount of spinach production was higher than average, even though with this high pH, spinach would not normally grow. This kind of phenomenon had been quite unthinkable before.

PINEAPPLES GROW DIFFERENTLY

Pineapples are one of the specialities of Okinawa. We experimented with soil conditioner and saw a difference in their growth. We had testing and control sections again. In the control section, we could see the ground because of fewer leaves. However, in the testing section, we could not see the ground at all because of the thick leaves and healthy growth of pineapples. We compared the roots as well. There were many roots on the pineapples in the testing section, whereas there were obviously fewer on the ones in the control section. (See Figure 8.5: Pineapple leaves were so thick in the testing section that we could not see the ground.).

KAIWARE RADISH SPROUTS PUSHED UP THE LID OF A PETRI DISH

We tested the germination of *kaiware* radish in testing plates with lids. In two plates we put seeds treated with tap water. In two other plates, we treated the seeds with Pi-Water. The ones treated with tap water rotted off, whereas the ones treated with Pi-Water grew, pushing the lids off. The difference in activation is obvious.

TEN-MINUTES IN PI-WATER MADE A DIFFERENCE IN POTATO GROWTH

The following experiment was done to treat potatoes with Pi-Water. We cut a seed potato in two and soaked one half in Pi-Water for 10 minutes and the other half in regular tap water. The difference in the number of roots sprouted was tremendous. The half soaked in Pi-Water had several times more roots than the other half soaked in tap water.

Potatoes are grown in the soil. Therefore, the more root each potato plant has, the more potatoes it will produce. Experts say that if you count the number of roots, then you would be able to find out how many potatoes it will produce. The half of the seed potato treated with Pi-Water for only 10 minutes grew to be extremely healthy compared to the other half that was not tested at all. Giving Pi-Water in this stage of potato budding makes a big

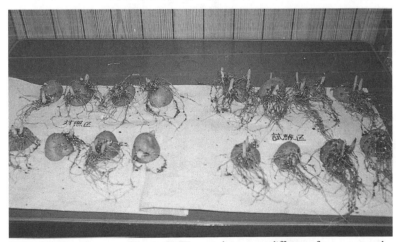

Figure 8.6: Ten minutes soaking in Pi-Water makes a great difference for most growth.

difference in its growth. (See Figure 8.6: Ten minutes soaking in Pi-Water makes a great difference for most growth.)

NO STAGNANT WATER IN THE PASSAGES OF
A STRAWBERRY GARDEN

A farmer in Saitama prefecture grew strawberries outside. We used Pi-Water soil conditioner in a testing section and grew strawberries in a conventional way in the control section. We checked both sections immediately after a rainfall, which is the best time for checking the soil. In the passages in the control section, there was some stagnant water from the rain. In the passages in the testing section, there was no water at all.

The above phenomenon occurred because of the particle combination in the soil treated with soil conditioner. In this testing section, the soil is ventilated, easily drained, and able to hold water well. It is worth paying attention to the fact that while it takes 200 to 300 years for aggregation to occur naturally, it only takes several weeks if we use Pi-Water soil conditioner.

MORE THAN TWICE AS MUCH RADISH WAS PRODUCED

We tested the production of radish in Gifu prefecture. We chose soil affected by a harmful bacterium called *fusarium* as a result of continuous usage (when soil loses its energy, these bacteria spread, causing plant stems to rot). In the testing section, we used soil conditioner, and in the control section we left the soil untreated. The index figure for the amount of good quality radishes produced was 100 for the control section and 240.8 in the testing section. Very few good quality radishes were produced in the control section.

PI-WATER OVERCOMES PROBLEMS CAUSED BY CONTINUOUS
SOIL USAGE IN GROWING TOMATOES

Tomatoes are one of the crops that are susceptible to problems caused by continuous usage of soil. If tomatoes are affected by these problems, they start to show bacterial wilt and fall down when they develop flower buds. Usually we try to solve this problem with grafting.

We did our experiment with a farmer in Gifu prefecture who had a greenhouse with this problem. We tried to let the tomatoes grow with their own roots without grafting. We only spread soil conditioner. Aogare disease, or bacterial wilt, did not occur; the crops were healthy. We tried to achieve similar results in other greenhouses with the same experiment. However, those experiments did not have the same results as the first one. The disease did not occur as much, but it still affected the tomatoes.

We also tried the experiment with melons. Unfortunately, it was impossible to grow them without grafting. However, these experiments indicated there is positive potential for Pi-Water in the future, which was the biggest achievement for us.

CORN WITH THICK STEMS AND STRONG ROOTS

In our experiment with corn, we soaked the testing section seeds in Pi-Water for 10 minutes. Only tap water was used in the control section. With this simple seed treatment, there was a big difference in the seeds' growth. The height of the corn in the testing and control sections was about the same. However, the stems of the corn in the testing section were very thick and spread left to right, and the roots grew much longer than we had expected. (See Figure 8.7: Significant growth of root in test section.)

Figure 8.7: Significant growth of root in test section.

MORE PEAS HARVESTED

We let peas soak in Pi-Water for 10 minutes prior to planting them in a testing section. As a result, we grew many peas. In the control section where peas were soaked only in tap water, we did not see any peas, although there were some flowers. Results of this experiment show that Pi-Water is more effective for reproductive growth rather than for nutritional growth.

DELICIOUS MELONS ORGANICALLY GROWN

We tried growing melons organically in Yamagata, Japan. Melon is extremely susceptible to diseases. Therefore, in the worst situation, we thought we might have to disinfect them twice a week. In our experiment, we applied only soil conditioner. We were ready to disinfect at any time, since we were afraid that disease might occur during the experiment. However, we were able to harvest the melons without having to disinfect them. They had minor diseases, but the diseases never spread.

TABLE 8.7 - FRESHNESS WEIGHT ONE MONTH AFTER SOWING

| | | FRESHNESS WEIGHT | | |
		ABOVE GROUND	BELOW GROUND	WHOLE PLANT (INDEX)
CORN	Control Section	204.9g	25.1g	230g (100)
	Test Section	554.7g	39.1g	593.8g (258)
FEJON	Control Section	93.9g	2.1g	69.0g (100)
	Test Section	149.7g	5.22g	154.9g (161)

Experiment conducted in Brazil - sowing March 17 - average weight of 15 stocks

THE WEIGHT OF INDIAN CORN DOUBLED

We tested Indian corn and *fejons* in Brazil. (See Table 8.7: Freshness Weight One Month after Sowing.) *Fejon,* a staple food for local people, belongs to the same family as the soybean. We measured the change in weight in respective plants. The Indian corn grown in the testing section weighed 2.4 times more than the corn grown in the control section. The *fejons* grown in the control section weighed 100 (index figure) whereas those grown in the testing section weighed 161. We could not compare the amount of production, as it was the beginning of winter there.

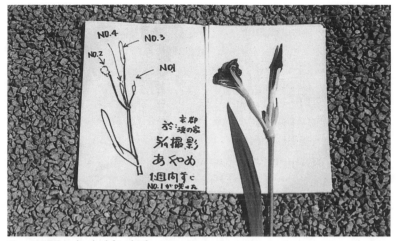

Figure 8.8: Iris that had four buds per stem.

FOUR IRIDES PER STEM

Continuous usage of the same soil normally does not affect iris. In the same pond, flowers will blossom year after year during the season. People enjoy seeing the iris in the iris garden in Kyoto every May and June. However, the number of stocks that do not spring up in the next season has increased over a long period of time. In this iris garden, we spread Pi-Water soil conditioner from above. As a result, there were very few stocks lacking flowers. At the same time, an unusual phenomenon occurred. Generally, the iris has two flowers per stem, but after we spread Pi-Water soil conditioner, there were four buds per stem. After the first two flowers fell, the third and fourth flowers blossomed. (See Figure 8.8: Iris that had four buds per stem.) At first we thought they might be deformed. However, we realized that iris initially had this much life energy. Up till that time the environment had not been good enough for the iris to demonstrate that energy.

HYACINTH WITH MANY MORE ROOTS

Pi-Water was applied to one hyacinth and tap water to the other. The roots of the plant grown in Pi-Water were so strong and numerous that we thought they might break the glass container.

As for the one treated with tap water, the roots were fewer in number and seemed quite weak in comparison.

Bulbs have nutrition inside, and a plant could live just on the nutrition within it. That is why giving Pi-Water information alone can make a big difference in growth.

A HALF-SPOILED DRACAENA STARTING TO SPROUT

The following experiment on the dracaena, commonly called "the plant of happiness," was done at a farm in Mie prefecture. The plants were put one by one into a pot for shipment. We applied Pi-Water to the testing section and used the ones grown under the usual method as the control section. The leaves of dracaena in the control section seem to be weak and hanging down. This is, however, how you would find dracaenas sold in stores. On the other hand, the dracaena in the testing section that was given Pi-Water and Pi-Water soil conditioner was full of energy and all the leaves were facing upward. (See Figure 8.9: Healthy dracaenas growing with Pi-Water and Figure 8.10: Dracaenas grown in the conventional way.) Experts say that they have only seen such dracaenas with so much energy in South America. We felt as if we received energy just by standing near these plants.

Figure 8.9: Healthy dracaenas growing with Pi-Water.

Figure 8.10: Dracaenas grown in the conventional way.

Normally, the farmer had to disinfect his dracaenas at least once a week. But after applying the Pi-Water system, he no longer needed to do so.

Generally when dracaenas are affected by a disease, we try to air the plants well and keep them dry. However, if Pi-Water is applied, you need to close the windows and spray Pi-Water to get rid of the diseases. Compared to the conventional method, Pi-Water application may seem difficult in learning the tricks of growing plants. However if you understand the characteristics of Pi-Water, it is not so difficult.

Importing dracaenas from Brazil or Costa Rica takes two months by boat. Therefore, some of plants rot during shipping. Once rotten, they must be disposed of, and when the dracaena is put in a greenhouse in Japan, the rotten ones must be separated from the healthy plants. The rotten ones are all burned to prevent the spread of disease to the healthy plants. However, no matter how the dracaenas are separated, occasionally rotten ones get mixed in with the healthy ones. When Pi-Water and Pi-Water soil conditioner are applied, however, the plants can be revived and start sprouting again.

Experts cannot believe these experiments. When they heard about them and saw what happened, they started testing Pi-Water, thinking that it might have a disinfecting function. They performed experiments to determine if Pi-Water had disinfecting capabilities but found that it does not. How can the fact that sprouts came out of a half rotten dracaena be explained? Pi-Water raised the life energy of the living part of the plant and then suppressed the increase of the bacteria. The fact that the plants did not continue to rot is just a secondary phenomenon.

ROADSIDE TREES DAMAGED BY SEA WATER AND SALTY BREEZE REGAIN HEALTH

When transplanting roadside trees, one must prune leaves well and wrap the roots with rope, which is labor intensive. Since transplanting the trees is a lot of work, workers thought about just pulling the trees out, replanting other trees, and applying Pi-

Figure 8.11: Salt damaged soil recovers with Pi-Water application.

Water. This was done as an experiment in Iwaki city in Fukushima prefecture, where the roadside trees are affected by sea water and salty breezes. The trees on the right side of the road were the testing section. Since this area is close to the ocean, roots do not stabilize very easily. However, applying Pi-Water solved the problem. (See Figure 8.11: Salt damaged soil recovers with Pi-Water application.)

BEAN SPROUTS CONTINUE TO GROW IN THE PACKAGE DURING SHIPPING

Bean sprouts are very delicate. They are put into plastic bags when shipped, which causes them to begin to rot at once. Bean sprouts grown with the Pi-Water system, however, continue to grow in the plastic bags.

A cubic shaped plant tub for bean sprouts is about 1.2 meters square and equally deep. The amount of oxygen the sprouts receive is different, depending on whether they are situated at the top, middle, or bottom of the container. The sprouts placed on the top part were discarded since they grew to be about 20 cm, and the ones in the middle and bottom parts were shipped.

A farmer in Hyogo prefecture grows bean sprouts using the Pi-Water system. They grow uniformly no matter in what part of the tub they are placed. Even at the bottom of the tub, there is never an oxygen deficiency problem.

If there is too much rain, the roots of the plants generally tend to rot. However, if the soil is treated with the Pi-Water system, the more it rains, the healthier the plants will become. We do not know how the roots obtain oxygen, but the way the bean sprouts on the top of the tub grow seems to suggest an answer to this question.

PI-WATER ALSO EFFECTIVE FOR MICROORGANISMS

A manufacturer in Nagano prefecture, Japan, tested Pi-Water's effect on microorganisms. The culture medium for Shimeji mushroom was in the test tube with Pi-Water information on top.

When a set amount of fungus is inserted into the tube, hyphae, the interwoven threads that form the mass of the fungus, normally expand toward the bottom of the tube, depending on the strength of the fungus. In the control tube, there was no Pi-Water information on the culture medium, so the hyphae grew to an area a little below the middle of the tube. The edge of the hyphae looked blurred and seemed to have dissolved in the middle. In the testing tube, the hyphae was definitely below the middle of the tube, reaching almost to the bottom. You can see clearly the edge of the hyphae and the medium. Thus, Pi-Water helps activate the microbe.

CHAPTER NINE

❋ ❋ ❋

APPLICATION OF PI-WATER IN THE STOCK BREEDING INDUSTRY

PI-WATER HELPS BRING HEALTHFUL MEAT TO THE TABLE

Pi-Water is very effective for the growth of animals. Farmers can raise their stock without relying on the medication and antibiotics they have previously had to use. The meat of the animals raised this way can be eaten without worries.

The following are some examples of how Pi-Water technology is applied.

YOUNG WEAK MICE BECAME HEALTHY AND GREW WELL

Young, weak mice were tested, and the changes that occurred were recorded. We gave newborn mice Pi-Water to drink and then checked their weight gain. They gained weight every day. When we let the mice drink Pi-Water twice a day, their weight increased more. When we injected Pi-Water into their abdomens, they gained even more weight. (See Graph 9.1: Growth Curves of Mice Given Pi-Water.)

HEALTHY PIGS AND NO MORE SMELLY PIG PEN

We did our experiment on a pig farm in Gifu prefecture, Japan. At some pig farms, an open system pig pen is used. In this system piglets are raised together in the same pens without changing their nursery beds until they are ready to be shipped,. You cannot dismiss this as an altogether old-fashioned method. It is said that engineers familiar with the latest technology in raising pigs have been closely studying this system recently.

Figure 9.1: Pigs in soil treated with Pi-Water.

GRAPH 9.1 - GROWTH CURVES OF MICE GIVEN PI-WATER

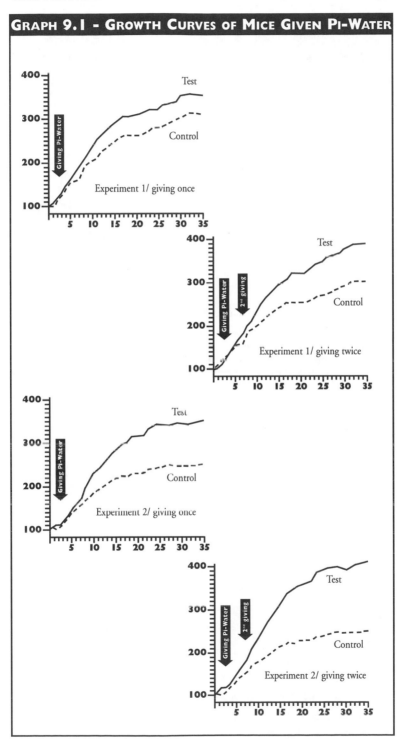

Unless farmers manage this open system carefully, they can have serious problems with odor, flies, and maggots. When we introduced the Pi-Water system into the floor covering of the pig pen and gave the pigs feed and water treated with Pi-water, no odor, flies, or maggots were present. (See Figure 9.1: Pigs in soil treated with Pi-Water.)

Foul odors occur because of fermentation caused by anaerobic bacteria. When Pi-information is added, it probably suppresses anaerobic fermentation and changes it to aerobic fermentation, which has no foul smell.

Aerobic fermentation produces a pleasant odor similar to bread baking. The characteristics of the smell change with the addition of Pi-information. Since flies and maggots live on the products of anaerobic fermentation, they cannot survive if the pattern of fermentation changes.

When we dissect pigs raised in the conventional way, we find that they have blood congestion in many places. The pigs seem healthy enough and do not appear to be suffering from any disease. Most pigs are in similar condition. Perhaps blood congestion is caused by the stress they suffer.

When we dissect a pig raised with Pi-Water system, we can see that its meat looks very clean, and there is no blood congestion. The quality of the meat is two grades higher.

Ham made from the meat of pigs raised with Pi-Water technology has a longer shelf life. A food company analyzed the meat in order to find out why it keeps for a long time. They studied various data, such as levels of amino and fatty acids. However, they could not find anything different from the regular pigs. They came up with the conclusion that the ham made from healthy pigs can keep for a long time. The fact is that the difference in living body energy causes such phenomena.

PIGS ON A DIET

When we gave piglets Pi-Water to drink, they grew in good health and were very active. Pigs seem to have four stages of growth. The piglets that had Pi-Water grew much faster than others. However, when they reached the mating stage, their growth stopped completely. The other pigs grew rapidly after the mating stage.

We doubted that their growth pattern changed because of having had Pi-Water. However, we were wrong. Pi-Water normalizes or balances the functions of living bodies, but it does not make them fatter.

The same applies to the growth pattern of human beings. In adolescence the human body tends to be slim and firm; so should the pigs. However, humans forced the pigs to keep gaining weight, thereby destroying the balance of their growth. It would not be surprising if the pigs suffered from diseases due to this artificial, accelerated growth. Pi-Water works in such a way that the natural growth of the animal was enhanced.

EGGS THAT CAUSE NO ALLERGIC REACTIONS

If we give hens Pi-Water to drink during their breeding season, they become much more productive. The Pi-Water system has already been applied in this industry just as in agriculture. Some of poultry raisers in Aichi and Gifu prefectures use drinking water and feed treated with the Pi-Water system. It is not necessary for them to use antibiotics to control their diseases. They have become very successful in raising healthy poultry. The taste and quality of the eggs improved and became just like the ones they used to produce a long time ago. (See Graph 9.2: Effect of Application of Pi-materials on Old Hens' Declining Egg Production.)

At the Inachi poultry farm in Toyohashi city, Aichi prefecture, farmers who are using this system report producing healthy eggs. They say, "The taste of the eggs improved tremendously after we began applying the Pi-Water system to poultry raising. We can pick up the egg yolk with our fingers without breaking it. Healthy hens means tasty eggs. Before we started using this system, the farm smelled so bad that we could smell it from about a kilometer away. Now we can smell the hens a little bit but nothing like it used to be. Before the Pi-Water system was introduced, if a hen died in the farm, we could tell where it was right away because of the terrible smell. Now, we cannot tell sometimes for a few days because there is much less odor. (See Figure 9.2: Introduction of

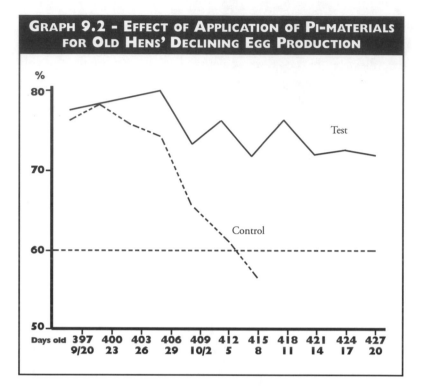

GRAPH 9.2 - EFFECT OF APPLICATION OF PI-MATERIALS FOR OLD HENS' DECLINING EGG PRODUCTION

Pi-Water in Poultry Farming Means Healthier Chickens, Greater Egg Production, and Reduced Smell.) And now the only reason hens die is because of accidents. None of them die from other causes. I was so pleased to receive a letter from people who are allergic to eggs, thanking me because they are now able to eat my eggs. People and poultry here both live healthy lives thanks to Pi-Water."

RAW EGGS REMAIN FRESH FOR TWO MONTHS
IN NORMAL TEMPERATURE

At poultry farms some eggs crack or break while they are being collected. Such eggs must be put at once into a container and sold to a food company. In summer, raw eggs tend to spoil easily, but it is difficult to store them very quickly.

We experimented with raw eggs to prove that Pi-Water has the ability to prevent spoiling. One of two transparent containers contained Pi-Water, and the other held regular tap water. We put

Figure 9.2: Introduction of Pi-Water in Poultry Farming Means
Healthier Chickens, Greater Egg Production, and Reduced Smell.

a raw egg in each and left them at room temperature. After two
months the egg in Pi-Water did not show any change. The one in
the tap water had spoiled completely, turning as white as milk.

AMAZING PRODUCTION RATE OF POULTRY

There is an amazing report that illustrates 99 percent effectiveness
in egg production rate. For example, we gave old hens Pi-Water to
drink and kept a record. Generally, the egg production rate of hens
drops after 400 days. If they stop laying eggs, the hens cannot be
sold for meat; not many people buy the meat of old hens these
days. But Pi-hens' meat continues to have excellent taste.

As we continued to have the hens drink Pi-Water, they continued to lay eggs—even after 900 days. Their eggs have a natural scent, reminding of us of the eggs we used to obtain 30 years
ago. We could also pinch the egg yolk with our fingers without
breaking it.

BLOOD DOES NOT COAGULATE

Pig's blood coagulates when it comes in contact with air, just like
human blood. However, when we added Pi-Water to pig's blood,
it did not coagulate for a long time. When we checked the pro-
thrombin time, a test that measures the time required for blood

to coagulate, we found that it took longer for blood with Pi-Water to coagulate than it did for untreated blood. When we mixed half-coagulated blood with Pi-Water, it turned back to its initial, uncoagulated state.

You might suppose that the blood of people who drink Pi-Water will not coagulate. On the contrary, applying Pi-Water to a bleeding cut quickly stops the bleeding. This sounds inconsistent, but these phenomena really occur.

If you consider Pi-Water as a medicine, you would misinterpret its properties. Pi-Water's aura energy raises human natural healing power, and as a result it stops bleeding faster.

PIG CELLS CONTINUE TO LIVE FOR SIX MONTHS IN PI-WATER

In order to see how cells are preserved in Pi-Water, we took a piece of lung from a pig that had just died and placed it in Pi-Water. Six months later it still maintained a bright pink color. All the cells from a control piece kept in regular tap water died within a couple of days. The sample began to rot and turn black, and the water became murky.

A similar thing happens when we use Pi-Water for fish. This is because of the information contained in the ferric/ferrous salt (aura energy) in the Pi-treated water, which influences the living cells.

CHAPTER TEN

✻ ✻ ✻

APPLICATION OF PI-WATER IN THE FISHING INDUSTRY

PI-WATER APPLIED TO THE FISHING INDUSTRY

We have seen the excellent effect that Pi-Water has on productive growth of plants and animals. Let me explain a few examples of its effectiveness in the aquaculture industry, an area that is getting a great deal of public attention because of the use of harmful chemicals.

EELS RAISED WITH PI-WATER RECEIVED JAPAN'S "BEST EEL AWARD"

We did an experiment on the growth of whitebait at an eel farm in Hamamatsu, Japan. We put 150 liters of Pi-Water into one 200-liter test water tank and well water into a control tank. Then we placed 30 whitebait (total weight 6.3 grams) in each tank.

Two months later the weight per whitebait was twice as heavy in the testing section as it was in the control section. Three months later it was three times as heavy. The whitebait were quite firm and not much different from freshly caught eels. (See Graph 10.1: Weight Change of Eel Fish.)

The thickness of the fish was obviously different. Those in the control section were about as thick as disposable chopsticks,

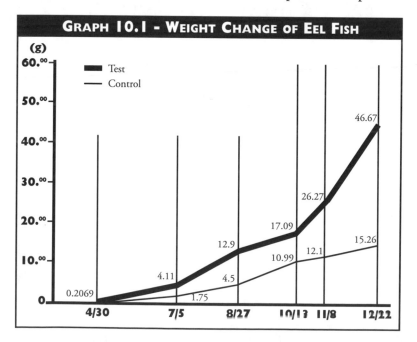

whereas the ones in the testing section were as thick as a little finger of an adult. We were quite surprised to see the difference. At about three months, we started to see a considerable increase in the weight of the whitebait.

A similar experiment was done in a big pond at a Kyushu eel farm. Eel from that pond tasted delicious; the meat was firm, and it could not be distinguished from eels that were naturally grown. This eel received the "Best Eel" in Japan award.

HORSE MACKERELS DO NOT SUFFER OXYGEN DEFICIENCY IN A CROWDED TANK

Mackerel is very sensitive to oxygen deficiency. When raising mackerel, there is a standard for how many fish can be put into one ton of water. We tested the ways Pi-Water could affect their condition.

At a fish farm in Saitama prefecture, we set up one two-ton tank with Pi-Water as a testing section and another with regular tap water as a control section. We put 100 mackerel into each tank and observed their condition for 10 days without changing the water. We did aeration only.

We picked out any dead fish as soon as we found them floating stomach up. If we waited until they actually died, the water would have become contaminated.

Within four days eight fish were floating in the control section, but none were floating in the Pi-Water testing section. Ten days later, there were 54 floaters in the control section and none in the

TABLE 10.1 - TESTS FOR CONDITIONS OF RAISING MACKERELS

	District	1st day	4th day	8th day	10th day
Condition of the fish	C	●	▲	▲	✖
	T	●	●	●	●
Condition of water	C	●	▲	✖	✖
	T	●	●	▲	▲
The fish floated	C	0	8	29	54
	T	0	0	0	0

C: Control section   T: Pi-Water treated section

●: good   ▲: not very good   ✖: bad

testing section. (See Table 10.1: Tests for Conditions of Raising Mackerels.)

As for the contamination of water, the testing section where Pi-Water was used did not become very contaminated. We also checked the health of the fish. The mackerel in the control section started to become a little abnormal after the fourth day. However, the fish in the testing section were quite healthy even after 10 days.

We could not help being surprised with the clear and obvious data, and we became suspicious. We did exactly the same experiment again under the same conditions because we thought we might have done something wrong. The result was exactly the same as the first time.

The above fact shows that Pi-Water can generate incredible results by raising the life power of living creatures.

LIVE FISH SYSTEM PRODUCES DELICIOUS SEAFOOD

We have seen that Pi-Water helps enhance the living energy and prevent weight loss of fish and shellfish. There is a Japanese restaurant named *Uotetsu* in Hazu town, Aichi prefecture, that takes advantage of the beneficial functions of Pi-Water. This restaurant follows a very simple system. They place a basket filled with Pi-ceramic in their fish tank and also keep Pi-ceramic in the recycle filter tank. When we asked the manager of the restaurant, Mr. Sakakibara, if such a simple device produced any effect, he said it has amazing effect.

FISH AND SHELLFISH ARE ALL HEALTHY AND CALM

When fish are stressed, they move around fast, but the fish at the restaurant remained calm in Pi-Water. Naturally, their death rate went down dramatically.

SHINING WATER

It is difficult to express with words how the water in the fish tank shines, but it does shine, which is different from just being transparent. A sensitive person seems to feel the softness of water just by putting a finger into the tank.

NOT NECESSARY TO CHANGE WATER

The fish tank water does not become contaminated. Therefore, it is now unnecessary to change it. It is sufficient to add sea water when necessary. The water was not been changed for more than six months.

NO FISHY SMELL

In a restaurant whose fish tank is not managed well, you smell a foul, fishy odor. This is considered to be a smell caused by weak fish emitting some kind of acid. Since *Uotetsu* started using this live fish Pi-Water system, they haven't experienced any fishy odor, which has helped upgrade the restaurant's image.

FARM-RAISED FISH TASTES NATURAL

Most of the fish now served at Japanese restaurants is raised in tanks. A true seafood lover can tell after one bite the difference between a naturally grown fish and one raised in a tank. However, when a tank-raised fish is put into the Pi-treated tank for three to four days, its meat becomes firm and the taste improves so much that one can hardly distinguish it from freshly caught fish.

NO WEIGHT LOSS OF CRAB

Weight loss is very common with crab meat. However, a king crab was placed in the Pi-treated tank for a month and lost hardly any weight. In addition, the meat was very firm. Generally, if crabs are kept in a tank for a long time, their meat becomes so soft that they cannot be used for customers.

A HORSE CRAB'S MEAT WEIGHT DID NOT DECREASE FOR FIVE DAYS

A fresh fish soaked in water treated by Pi-Water can be kept fresh for a long time. However, the soaking must be done right after the fish is caught. It is essential that the organs or cells of the fish themselves are alive in order to produce the proper effect.

In Erimo-cho, Hokkaido, we tested a horse crab in front of a fisherman with several decades of fishing experience. When we catch a horse crab in winter with the temperature at about −15C, it is half-dead. Once a crab is in such condition, it is said that it cannot be revived because its cells are damaged when it freezes.

However, when we placed a half-dead crab in the water containing Pi-Water, it came back to life again.

A horse crab normally loses 30 to 40 percent of its meat after three to four days. So, we tested to see how much meat it would lose with Pi-Water treatment.

We tested four crabs, A, B, C, and D. We soaked them all in Pi-Water and weighed them each day for five days. Crab A weighed 580 g on January 26 and 750 g on February 1. B weighed 450 g and did not lose any weight for five days. C weighed 540 g and did not lose any weight. D weighed 470 g and lost only 5 g. If you use the Pi-Water system, you can eat fresh crab in Tokyo.

TUNA KEPT FOR 40 DAYS AT 0°C CAN BE EATEN AS SASHIMI (RAW FISH)

We tested the preservation of freshness of flatfish. We treated flatfish with Pi-Water, wrapped it with plastic wrap, and kept it at 5°C.

Fifteen days later, the flatfish in the control section began to spoil and bleed. However, the fish in the testing section was still fresh. Then we decided to measure the freshness of each flatfish. Generally freshness is measured by the unit called K value. The smaller the number, the fresher the fish is. Sashimi is usually very good if its K value measures from zero to 30. If it is more than 60, the fish is not edible. This is one kind of test.

The K value of the flatfish in the control section was 0. Fish with that K value is impossible to eat even if you bake or boil it. On the other hand, K value of the flatfish in the testing section was about 40, which means it was edible if baked or boiled.

There is a variety of tuna called *kimeji maguro,* which is very small. We tested several by keeping them for 40 days in ice water at 0°C. The ones preserved in Pi-Water were edible as sashimi after 40 days. The ones in regular water were completely rotten.

INSHORE TUNA AND GURUKUN, A SPECIALTY OF OKINAWA PREFECTURE

We tested inshore tuna, this time keeping them in ice water at 0°C for 20 days. The color of the gills of the fish not treated with

Pi-Water became dull. However, the color of the gills of the fish in the Pi-Water still looked fresh, as if they were just caught.

A fish called *gurukun* from Okinawa is a very difficult fish to preserve. It is designated as a prefectural fish of Okinawa and tastes very good. Unfortunately, people in the main islands are unable to enjoy them since they change color within 30 to 40 minutes after they are caught. Freezing them would dry their meat so much that they could not be served. No matter how hard fishermen have tried, they have not been able to ship *gurukun* out of Okinawa.

The Pi-Water system turned the impossible into the possible. At first, we thought we were just lucky. But we repeated our experiments and always had satisfactory results without any failure.

FOODS DO NOT SPOIL BUT, INSTEAD, IMPROVE IN TASTE

Pi-Water is not perfect. If there are the best conditions, amazing results can be achieved. However, the following experiments have had uneven results. Nevertheless, I believe Pi-Water will be effective in several foods for future consumers.

As for the preservation of freshness, we have complete data for fresh fish. However, it is still unknown to us how well we can preserve objects in plastic wraps.

We treated plastic wraps used at home with Pi and made that our testing section. We wrapped strawberries in the plastic wraps. The control portions spoiled and turned black. The testing section strawberries did rot, but with white molds. We think that the air inside the treated wrap and the bacteria flora must have changed.

SOY SAUCE DOES NOT SPOIL

Some soy sauce is produced without preservatives or any other additives. If we dilute it with water, it starts to spoil right away. However, if we treat it with Pi-Water it will not spoil.

MILK DOES NOT SPOIL

We put milk in four small containers. Two of them were treated with Pi-water, and the other two were without treatment. These

TABLE 10.2 - COFFEE TASTE TEST RESULTS				
ORIGINAL BEANS	ITEMS	TREATED GROUP A	TREATED GROUP B	TREATED GROUP C	CONTROL D
Riozona	Acidity	-	-	-	+
	Mildness	+	+	+	-
	Rio Smell	++	++	++	+
Riado	Acidity	-	-	-	+
	Mildness	+	+	+	-
	Aroma	++	++	++	+
Mineiro	Acidity	-	-	-	+
	Mildness	+	+	++	+
	Aroma	+++	+++	+++	++

NOTE:

(1)   For rio smell (iodine smell), the more +s there are, the worse the smell is.

(2)   For aroma, the more +s there are, the better the smell is.

containers were left for several days. The untreated milk spoiled or separated.

PROFESSIONAL PEOPLE WERE AMAZED AT COFFEE'S TASTE

We tested the taste of regular coffee at a large instant coffee manufacturer in Brazil. The purpose of this test was to see whether tasty coffee could be made from beans that are not very good. The people who tested the taste were seven nationally certified seven evaluators.

We used beans such as *riozona* and *riado,* which were not good quality. Low quality beans have an acid, iodine smell and a stinging taste. Iodine is good for your health, but in a favorite drink, it is a problem. We made coffee out of these beans, using water containing 10 percent, 1 percent, and 0. 1 percent Pi-water.

All of the coffees became very mild. The acid, stinging taste disappeared. This did not have anything to do with the Pi-water concentration rate. To our surprise, the smell of iodine increased from +1 to +2. I was astonished to see that all the evaluators reached the same conclusion. (See Table 10.2: Coffee Taste Test Results.)

Now that the problem of the taste is completely solved, we need to address the problem of the smell. I'm sure with time we win be able to solve that problem too.

You can also add Pi-Water to cheap wine, rice wine, whisky, or any other beverage, and it will produce a milder taste.

AFTERWORD

❁ ❁ ❁

I sincerely wish to nurture this new technology, Pi-Water, with the kind support and cooperation of many people of good will. I would like to ask for your support.

For your information, this book has not been written for the purpose of scientific studies. I did my best to be accurate with the information presented. However, I also have some bold hypotheses. Please keep this in mind when you read it.

I would like to take this opportunity to pay my deepest respects to the late Dr. Yoshiaki Goto of Nagoya University, who was a pioneer in the study of Pi-Water, and Dr. Shoji Yamashita, who developed Dr. Goto's studies.

The studies of Pi-Water have been supported and helped by a number of people. We managed to come this far thanks to their support and help. I would like to express my sincere gratitude to Mr. Toshihiko Chibana of the Environmental Protection Institute.

I would also like to thank Mr. Kunio Akiyama of Rexpress and Ms. Satoko Itabashi of Kosaido Publishing, who encouraged me and led me to the completion of this book Their cooperation has been tremendous.

SHINJI MAKINO, PH.D.